A Hymn of Changes:

Contemplations of the I Ching

by

David LaChapelle

Ragged Sky Press
Princeton, NJ

Dedicated to the Great Mystery
flowing through our lives,

and to all expressions of the Divine
appearing as Teacher.

In honor of David La Chapelle for his endless service, compassion and wisdom. This book is one of his greatest gifts to students of life, consciousness and transformation. May you be spoken to, and may the unfolding of your life be guided and refined through its wisdom.   - The *Hymn of Changes* re-publication group

Contents

Foreword

As a child, I was nurtured and sustained by nature. I was raised in Alta, Utah, in the winters (one of the oldest ski resorts in the country), and spent the summers on my father's research project in the Olympic National Park in Washington State. As early as three years old, I was climbing peaks and wandering on glaciers. My time was spent watching the sun rise over the sensuous curves of glaciers and sink into the Pacific with the lingering smell of fir trees carried by the thermals from the forests below. I remember playing by myself in the midst of such beauty, feeling a curious sense of well-being and completeness.

Several years ago I returned to Mount Olympus, the home of the gods. It had been over ten years since I had seen the home of my childhood. Standing once again on the edge of my childhood paradise, I was overwhelmed by the beauty. I remember thinking as I looked out over the glaciers I loved, "Nothing I could ever do in my life could match this." Immediately after having that thought a sudden impulse occurred to me: I knew I should go back down off the mountain and paint images for the I Ching. Never in my life has an inspiration come so directly and with so little warning.

I had used the I Ching in my late teens and early twenties. For a time I had even read from it daily. But it had been years since I had really connected with the I Ching, and now, on the threshold of my spiritual home, I was once again brought back to an ancient book of wisdom which transcends culture, time, and place.

I returned from the mountain and began an intensive period of painting, which lasted for several months. Exactly nine months later I finished the series of 64 paintings. As a support for each of them, I composed brief commentaries on each of the hexagrams. These initial commentaries were written one afternoon in Rocky Mountain National Park under a ponderosa pine tree. These descriptions contained the seeds of this present book and can be found on the face pages.

During the painting process I had a dream in which the purpose of the images was announced in the form of the hexagram Grace. Grace is composed of the two trigrams: The Clinging (Fire) and Keeping Still (Mountain). The clarity of Fire dances upon the majesty and stillness of the Mountain. This is emblematic of the beauty or Grace of art: the purpose of art is to still the mind and take the viewer to the edge of their own soul. Art alone cannot do your inner work, but it can inspire and set the stage for profound spiritual contact. This is my hope in terms of the images presented in this book. It is an invitation to the reader to take a leap into their own spiritual

path as reflected by the eternal wisdom of the I Ching.

The commentaries in this book reflect two strong currents in my own life: my rootedness in nature, and my studies and investigations of psychological and spiritual growth. I have attempted to make the hexagrams more accessible to our everyday experience. I found that as I wrote the commentaries they were feeling more like hymns than a scholarly exposition, and I share them in that spirit. The hexagrams are elegant descriptions of inner cycles within our growth and are of enormous comfort and support in our journey. May you enjoy your journey through them.

Thanks to Linda Lockridge and Shoshana Seligman for dedicated editing. Thanks to Sharon Toner for midwifery. Thanks to all who have shared their lives with me; this has made it all real. A special thanks to my wife (Shar Fox) for her support, love and patience. Thanks to my parents for giving me the gift of a nature-blessed childhood.

- David LaChapelle, as originally printed, 1991

"Ascending" I Ching Painting by David

Acknowledgments

This newly revised edition of *A Hymn of Changes* was lovingly brought forward through the collective efforts of: Catherine Baumgardner, who transcribed the entire manuscript from the one original copy at hand, during a retreat in Hawaii 2006; as well as Barbara and Michael Cecil, Cynthia Yoder, Yvonna Leutzinger, Paul and Carol Hwoschinsky, and Alexis and Carlos Delgado, who creatively brainstormed during David's illness on how to organize an income stream for medical expenses from his extensive intellectual asset base. The idea for this production was graciously received by friends and family with great support, following a skillful letter from Barbara Cecil, which really got the ball moving. The focus of this group's intention offered David an enormous gift of posterity and legacy through this reprinting. He had time to create the cover layout himself and to guide Devin Hormann-Rivard in the early stages of the process.

Devin is responsible for the most time-consuming leg of the publication cycle: the actual layout and formatting of the new edition. Without his heartful dedication, this project never would have materialized. He faced the additional difficulties of applying himself to a very steep learning curve in a new computer layout program, as well as holding remarkably steady form through the difficult loss of his dear friend and spiritual teacher.

Lisa Van de Water, Lisa McLaren, and Cheryl Foley contributed enormously by combing through, multiple times each, with precision and eagle-eye editing skills. May you feel their care throughout. I and countless selfless beings contributed with additional editing, organizational and design skills, as well as financial support. This edition is another step closer, but in no way represents the full potential awaiting this book. David created a unique painting for each of the 64 hexagrams and then I came across the long-lost photo slides of them after he passed. It is my and Devin's hope to continue refining the text and eventually publish a full-color version with the hexagrams each augmented with its particular painting. It is with this in mind, your feedback and corrections are warmly welcomed and appreciated.

Ananda Elise Foley,
companion, loving friend forever

At Play in the Fields of the Universe...

Traditional means of using the I Ching have included some sort of divinatory activity. A division of yarrow stalks (or throw of three coins) became a meditation on the nature of change. How can a simple throw of coins or division of yarrow stalks possibly be a true indicator of one's deep emotional and spiritual state? The skeptical mind sees this as a parlor game or a cheap magical trick. How can a simple probability of "yes" or "no" events shape a meaningful answer?

In answering these questions it is useful to consider field theory. A field, according to the definition given in physics text books, is a "condition" in space which causes two oppositely charged particles to interact with one another without touching. Electricity, magnetism, and light are the most common fields that we encounter in our daily world. The crucial concept at work here is that, given sufficient potential energy, interactions can take place between two entities without any visible physical contact.

The concept of force fields are recorded in Yogic literature which predates modern physics by thousands of years. According to Yogic systems of inquiry each individual is made up of a series of interpenetrating "bodies" which have differing characteristics depending on which "body" is being considered. The subtle bodies are force fields which interact with other energies of non-physical nature. Thus contact with Divinity is actually described in Yogic texts as coming to experience the "knower of the fields." Direct spiritual experience is described as an interaction between the individual and the Divine by way of these subtle "bodies" or fields.

Consider for a moment a vision of our solar system from a perspective of energy fields. Instead of a Newtonian concept of a hard ball of energy at the center of our solar system spewing out little arrows of light, a field-oriented conception of the sun sees it as a vast center of a multidimensional space/time waveform generator. Waves and waves of energy dancing in many dimensions form the womb of the solar system. These waves move across space and "collapse" into discrete energies of photons as they interact with our planetary surface. This collapse means that the waveform nature of light has changed and that light now acts as a discrete particle, interacting with matter on the earth in a quite predictable way. This peculiar quality of light was one of the anomalies which led to modern quantum physics. What was once a diffuse wave, when interacting with solid matter takes on the characteristics of matter. This is quite fortunate for us because this behavior of light is directly responsible for our being able to see in the physical world.

Extending the idea of a field beyond the physical world we could think of every psyche as having a field of energy associated with its functioning. The ability to "see" in this realm is dependent on being able to make a meaningful contact with these fields. Numerous examples of people knowing when the phone rings who is calling, or, thinking of a long-lost friend the day they suddenly appear, can be explained if one thinks in terms of a field of energy being associated with individuals instead of them just occupying the limited space of their bodies. This field of energy is of a nonphysical nature and is not bound by time or space. The ability to sense people before they actually make contact physically happens because their field has made contact with the delicate sensing mechanisms of our body/mind. This contact is transformed into meaningful information, much as the sun's energy becomes discrete in the collapse of the wave-form nature of a photon. A mental picture or a feeling of that person will suddenly become apparent as the field "collapses" and takes form in our body/mind.

Another approach to understanding field theory is contained in the following story. This story is attributed to Richard Wilhelm, a translator of the I Ching who lived and traveled in China in the early part of this century. The eminent Swiss psychologist, Carl Jung required his close students to tell this story before the start of any seminar in order to set a proper tone for the investigations of his work. The story is as follows:

Richard Wilhelm was wandering in China and had heard of an area which was experiencing a severe drought. He had heard that the villagers had pooled their money and had paid for a Taoist Rainmaker to come and help end the drought. Richard, who was interested in such matters, traveled to the village to see if in fact this Rainmaker was able to do as he said.

The Rainmaker arrived, wandered about the village for a time and then asked for a shelter to meditate in. He meditated for three days, and at the end of three days not only did it start raining, but it snowed, an event that was unheard of for that time of the year.

When Richard asked the Rainmaker how he had succeeded in ending the drought the rainmaker looked at him quizzically and replied,

"I did not make the snow, I am not responsible."

"But what have you done these three days?"

"Oh, I can explain that. I come from another country where things are in order. Here they are out of order, they are not as they should be by the ordinance of heaven. Therefore the whole country is not in Tao, and I also am not in the natural order of things because I am in a disordered country. So I had to wait three days until I was back in Tao and then naturally the rain came."

Implicit in the story is the idea that with sufficient spiritual awareness we are able to affect our environment much as a field of energy radiates from a source of light. The Rainmaker made rain by making himself whole, and in doing so made his environment whole. (This, by the way, is one of the central ideas to be found in the I Ching). We could extend our analogy of the waveform solar system to the meditating Taoist master. He becomes the "sun" as he meditates. Waves of multi-dimensional energy radiate from him and help synchronize the natural world. It is not his own will which achieves this tremendous change, but his ability to link his personal field of being with the larger resonant field of the Tao.

The idea of field interaction is quite useful when postulating an explanation for how the I Ching works. When an individual is formulating a question they are actually meditating inasmuch as their mind becomes focused. This focus creates an intensification of their mental/emotional/spiritual field. As they throw the coins the field collapses and takes form as the individual lines of the hexagram (analogous to the collapse of the waveform nature of light into particles as light interacts with matter).

An example of this happened at a workshop I was giving on the I Ching. One of the women in the group had asked a question and was throwing the coins as everyone else looked on. Another woman, who was observing, reported that she knew before each throw exactly what the woman would throw, line for line. From the model we are working with, this indicates that a field of energy had already formed which someone who is sensitive enough can actually pick up and register as an impression before the coins are even thrown. The seemingly random toss of the coins actually is influenced by the intensity of the field of each person's consciousness. In this light the skeptical mind will create a low-energy field which registers a seemingly random throw, whereas a mind focused and open will create the energy to organize a meaningful and significant answer.

The I Ching throws are much more than a simple divination device. They are a training system designed to instruct the user in the interaction of subtle force fields with the physical world. The act of throwing the hexagram helps an individual become more aware of this interaction. Inasmuch as the I Ching may be a code of universal structures, it is a language which names the very subtle and often hidden patterns in our lives. Revealing hidden matrices is one of the fundamental functions of the I Ching. This act of field organization is as important as the answer itself. The repeated contemplation of symbols, which speak of fundamental energy transformations, begins to act as a feedback system which helps reorganize the psyche around these core images. As the psyche becomes more organized, its field intensifies, so to speak, then the ability to penetrate into the subtleties of the Tao becomes a possibility. This is the spiritual practice of the I Ching: a training in life itself.

Extended use of the I Ching is a study in the possible permutations of life. By relating to the hexagrams on an ongoing basis, the I Ching trains the user to sense the flow of events as they unfold much as a good martial artist will sense the patterns of his opponent. The changing lines in the hexagrams form the gateway to each transformation. For example, in consulting the I Ching about the writing of this book I threw *Retreat*: Mountain over Heaven with five changing lines which produces *Decrease*:

9

Lake under Mountain. The I Ching is saying that in order to write successfully I need a period of retreat, which is a systematic withdrawal from the world. There is an accumulation of insight and power based on a retreat which is necessary in order to write. The result of this retreat will be found in *Decrease*, a lovely hexagram when describing the writing process. The image associated with *Decrease* is of a lake under a mountain. The waters of the lake are able to distill the essential qualities of the environment and reflect them in a way in which the universal can be made approachable and within the grasp of our daily experience. The process of writing is not unlike the reflections on a lake: capturing the grandeur of a mountain in the ripples of a few lines of prose.

The transformation of *Retreat* into *Decrease* shows me one of the possible outcomes of a retreat. A different moment will bring a different changing line, (or lines) with a new hexagram, pointing the way in a new direction. Each of the hexagrams is a window which opens to many other possibilities. After using the I Ching over time, one's mind begins to be trained in this possibility of ever-changing states of feeling, experience and insight. One of the results of this training is a capacity to tolerate change and stay open to the movement of life. Instead of guarding against negativity and creating walls and barriers, which often backfire as fear and separation, you are able to perceive the underlying guidance of a wisdom which encompasses change and opens ever outward to life and its lessons.

Each life event is then seen as a window in time which opens to a new possibility. Some may feel negative, some may feel positive, but underneath the momentary reaction is a process of development which is an emanation of a deeper matrix: the ground of our lives. This fundamental ground is named by the different traditions: It is "our father's will" of the Christian tradition, it is the "unstruck sound" of the Zen Buddhists, it is the "Spirit which always moves" of the Sioux, and it is the "Tao" of the Chinese schools of philosophy. This fundamental ground is not accessible to our rational minds and is often obscured by fears and doubts.

The I Ching has the power to help us turn over each event in our lives and uncover the roots of its formation and the direction of its flow. This constant uncovering process strips away false understanding and refines our intuitive grasp of the unseen matrix of the world. Seen from this perspective, the world is not an a causal body of accidents, but a web of interconnected events which weave a body of being. This web of being is alive and scintillating. There is a quality of adventure as we follow the hidden pathways of this fundamental tapestry which can neutralize many of our negative emotions. Lethargy, fear, doubt and despair are replaced by an upwelling feeling of belonging, of guidance and purpose. Indeed, one of the early translations of the word *Ching* meant the warp upon which a weaving is formed. The I Ching laid down the underlying pattern of universal principles upon which the individual was asked to weave the tapestry of their own experience. In the process of joining the personal to the universal an understanding of the Tao emerges which is more profound than a mere intellectual exercise; it is a process of spiritual transformation.

Gentle Stillness

Many people who approach the I Ching are motivated by some confusion or question relating to their personal lives. The I Ching offers a distillation of psychological and spiritual wisdom in response to their questions. This wisdom is rooted in a fundamental understanding of patterns in the natural universe. This knowledge is difficult to communicate in a linear, verbal manner, which is precisely why the I Ching is designed in the manner that it is: a multi leveled text of number, form, image, and commentary.

The numeric elegance of the book has been a source of wonder for mathematicians dating, in the West, all the way back to Leibnitz, the father of binary mathematics. In fact, Leibnitz was sent a copy of the I Ching by Jesuit missionaries in China and the text was helpful in his formulation of binary mathematics. The fact that modern day computer science is based on a binary code is no mere coincidence. It speaks of the universality of the hexagrams as a language which is essential to the structure of nature and the human mind.

The I Ching's ability to synthesize numeric and metaphoric content into a meaningful whole is part of the reason it is so effective as a guide for inner work. The abstract realm of numbers is linked to the real world of cause and effect through the binary code of the hexagrams. The hexagrams present a pattern of binary pulses which are then linked to an image and a commentary. Often the spatial array of the binary code is used as an anchor for the meaning of the hexagram. Thus in the hexagram The Corners of the Mouth (Nourishment), the actual shape of the hexagram mimics the shape of the human mouth. More often the binary code describes a slice of time which has a particular configuration of energy. This process of constructing reality based on a binary system is found in our own nervous system and is mirrored in our modern world by digital sound and video imagery.

Many philosophers throughout history have considered numbers to be the most pure expression of spiritual reality. The Greek philosopher Pythagoras said, "All is arranged according to number." The great cathedrals and temples of the world are physical embodiments of the power of numbers. The great domes, vaults, and arches are all describing the precise relationships of mathematical equations. The I Ching, also known as The Book of Changes, allows us to link up the realm of numerical codes with psychological and spiritual wisdom. Through the shifting of the lines from yin to yang, we derive one hexagram from another. This creates a pattern of change which allows the reader to experience the actual transformation which has occurred numerically. Modern physics has developed similar structures called event lines: charts of transformations which determine action in the physical world.

Linked to the binary system of the I Ching are images. The use of images allows the reader to invoke the powers of visualization in determining the meaning of the hexagram. The use of imagery accesses parts of the mind/body which cannot be brought into use by either number or word. The imagery of the I Ching is derived directly from our daily world: The Mountain, Lake, Wind, Thunder, Earth, Water, Fire and Heaven. The elements of the natural world become the ciphers to depict the construct of our inner world. This translation of outer image to inner symbol is so organic that we find ourselves able to contemplate quite abstract ideas with the grounding of earth-based imagery. It is precisely this ability to deal with the abstract in such a concrete manner that allows the I Ching to be such a wise guide. Hexagrams will, in a moment, depict the more universal pattern at work in a given situation.

The hexagrams can also be useful in confirming the direction of our inner work. One such example involves three women of Jewish ancestry who were working with the myth of the Wandering Jew. The three were part of a group that had gathered for the purpose of spiritual retreat. In examining the fundamental homelessness of the Jewish people, what we see is that for close to eighteen hundred years they were coming to grips with their own inability to settle down, form meaningful relationships and establish permanent homes. As part of a process before leaving for solo time, all thirteen participants of the group threw hexagrams to help clarify their purpose in going on Retreat. The three women threw the same hexagram: The Wanderer. The process of seeing objectively the same hexagram mirroring each woman's inner question was quite helpful in placing their work in a larger context. Understanding the nature of The Wanderer enabled the participants to realize that what they were experiencing in their own lives was indeed shared by others. The ability of the I Ching to reflect accurately the inner work of all three women was a vital and living sign of a larger pattern at work. It is, particularly, this ability to remind us of the greater picture that is one of the I Ching's greatest strengths.

There is a fundamental schism between the East and the West regarding the method for dealing with personal pain. The East has a bias away from the individual and towards the universal: life is suffering, seek the great path of liberation; all is Karma, all is Grace; what can you do but pray and practice? Whereas the West will counter with the anthem of the individual: you have the power to change your life; take charge and make it happen! One path leads to an anemic expression of personal power, and the other to the carnage and violence of Western exploitation, where the individual is paramount and ignores the needs of the greater environment. The I Ching, though rooted in the East, offers a synthesis of these two world views. It offers a clear vision of the universal and the individual's relationship to the whole, and yet, at the same time, has practical and immediate advice about current problems. With gentle stillness the hexagrams unravel the intricate issues of our lives and help place each event in the matrix of an ever-changing, yet fundamentally whole, fabric of life.

For example, a woman who was healing a wound left from an abortion and grappling with how to express her sexuality received the following Hexagrams:

Deliverance: Thunder over Water, changing to *Unknowing*: Water under Mountain. *Deliverance* marks a dramatic shift of events essentially as an act of Grace. Lightning falls from above and electrifies a body of Water like a flash of awareness, charging the watery realm of sexual energies and subconscious urges. There is a Deliverance from a long period of turbulence and this Deliverance is not based upon self-effort. It is simply a stroke of lightning from above. *Deliverance* changes to *Unknowing* (*Youthful Folly*). Here Water springs from a mountain and plunges headfirst in the abyss. There is great courage present as well as a quality of youthfulness which could be dangerous. There is no way to stop a spring from flowing; it follows the dictates of gravity and flows without regard to its future.

In analyzing the woman's hexagrams we find the following information forthcoming: the woman must deal with her sexuality and the powerful force it exerts, but there is a quality of unknowing involved which means that she must take the plunge realizing that she cannot consciously understand all that is involved. In *Keeping Still* (The Mountain), the upper trigram of the hexagram *Unknowing*, there is an implicit hint as to how to guide her actions. The Mountain is symbolic of a still, quiet mind that does not cogitate over actions, but remains strong and intuitively aware. From such a place in herself she will know how to respond to the dangers of the journey and her youthfulness will be restored.

Diagramed by the two hexagrams is a clear progression of the woman's process. A period of intense mental activity (Thunder) associated with an emotional/sexual issue (Water) then transforms to a quiet inner strength (Mountain) balanced by a youthful exuberance and possible danger (Water again). The I Ching does not pretend to say it will be an easy journey, but it is one she must take; she has no choice. Her Deliverance (a universal function) is followed by advice on how to explore her own nature: a deeper plunge into her sexual and emotional nature. It is a clear statement that she needs to release the past pain and accept Deliverance from the situation as a gift, and then take the plunge into her own sexual nature by cultivating her inner stillness and meditating more.

Over and over again as the hexagrams transform into each other, we find a constant cycling of self-action and surrender to the movement of the Tao. This interweaving of self-generated activity and fundamental ground-of-being provides a gentle yet powerful way of gaining insight into life situations. Implicit in the world view of the I Ching is a sense of fundamental connection between the personal and the universal. Each of the hexagrams, in its own way, becomes a mirror of this process. The first two hexagrams, *The Creative* and *The Receptive*, set the stage for this dance. *The Creative* is an impulse which originates deep in the heart of the Tao and emerges to interact with the personal world of *The Receptive*.

From this perspective, every event in our lives is seen as a mixture of the two realms. Recognizing this and harmonizing our actions with the appropriate movement of the moment is one of the fundamental lessons of the I Ching. There are times to let go and trust the greater flow, and then there are times when direct and immediate personal action is called for. This ability to make the right judgment in a given situation is symbolized by the Sage. The hexagrams elegantly guide us through a myriad world of the permutations of these two basic aspects of nature. As one hexagram forms into the next from situation to situation, we began to gain an intuitive grasp of the fabric of our worlds, and just how the individual and the universal are the same and yet different.

The ability to penetrate beyond the immediate reactionary world of cause and effect, judgment and criticism, and come to a recognition of the Tao at work in each situation is fostered by the I Ching. This is not some magical trick or blind act of faith. It is a profound entrainment and synchronization of verbal, visual, and mathematical patterns which gestalt into a fundamental weaving of reality. The greater our ability to recognize whole patterns, the more likely we are to navigate our lives in response to the fundamental chords of existence.

Anchored in the depths of the Tao, our lives become an expression of that wisdom and not a struggle to overcome the endless obstacles of daily living. The shifting form of the hexagrams guides us through the innumerable situations of our lives by showing us the footprints of the Gods. These footprints are the matrix of universal archetypes which guide the path of life. Upon them, we can walk a bit more confidently with the Book of Changes as our friend.

The Temple of the Changes

When working with the Book of Changes it is useful to visualize a correspondence between the trigrams (or basic alphabet of the I Ching) and the human body. The concept of linking abstract ideas and symbols to parts of the human body is found historically in all major cultural traditions.

Ayurvedic medicine, formulated several thousand years ago in India, considered the fundamental health of our bodies to be an interaction of basic qualities which they named Earth, Water, Fire, Air and Space. The Hermetic tradition, based on teachings from Egypt and Greece, has a similar classification. Modern chemistry, which has its antecedents in the alchemical world of the Middle Ages, is actually not so far removed from this nomenclature of physical reality . If we look at the natural world we clearly see these various realms depicted. A low-energy system in which the atomic structure is locked into a defined matrix produces Earth. As energy is introduced into the system, the molecules begin to vibrate until the melting point of any solid is reached: Water. If more energy is delivered, then the fluid state vaporizes and we have the realm of Air.

To understand Space as a concept we need to jump disciplines for a moment and consider quantum physics. One of the latest formulations in this field, known as zero point physics, posits that there is a vast field of energy which permeates Space. There are current theories which point to an implicit reliance of the hydrogen atom upon the dynamic exchange of energies with this field. In other. words, this fundamental field may, in fact, be sustaining hydrogen, which is a basic building block of our known physical world. This underlying field, which extends between planets as well as earth-bound objects, is what is referred to as 'Space' by the ancients. This fundamental field is the energy source out of which the other elements precipitate in order to create the physical world we know.

We have five trigrams from which the analogy of the elemental model of reality can be readily made: The Receptive as Earth, The Abysmal as Water, The Clinging as Fire, The Gentle Wind as Air, and the Creative (Heaven) as Space.

Earth is associated with the base of the spine and has psychological correlates in issues of survival, basic fears, and maintenance of the physical plane.

Water is associated with the pelvis and is considered the medium of emotions. Desire, both sexual and otherwise, is attributable to this trigram.

Fire is associated with the solar plexus and is linked to issues of power and personal expression. Self-determination and inner Fire are its hallmarks. (Interestingly, in ayurvedic medicine, this Fire is considered the driving mechanism for vision).

Air is associated with the chest area and deals with issues of love, compassion, and understanding. Love can penetrate all boundaries, hence the description "penetrating" for The Gentle Wind.

And finally Heaven, The Creative, is linked with the source of inspiration which flows downwards from above our heads. Divine inspiration and insight are the domain of this realm.

The remaining three trigrams describe psychological and spiritual functions, and are linked in the body to the head and neck.

A Lake reflects the Heavens and makes known on Earth what is occurring in the Heavens. This act of expression is central to its function. As the throat is the seat of expression, it is a natural correspondence for The Joyous Lake.

Thoughts appear with lightning-like quickness in our minds. This movement of thought is the basis of intelligence and has, in many esoteric traditions, been associated with the element Fire. Thunder, in this context, is identified with the mind and the activity of our intellect. Its bodily correspondence is above and behind the eyes.

The stillness which comes with meditation is necessary to uncover more fundamental layers of being. This idea of a quiet mind in which the whispers of the soul can be heard is associated with The Mountain. This quality is associated with an awakened mind and has its bodily correlate in the higher brain centers. This is the trigram that denotes deep meditation in which the top of the head opens and it we are able to communicate with the Heavens. The Hopis have pictographs of prayer which display wavy lines emanating from the top of their heads as symbolic of this process.

The hexagrams are depictions of these fundamental forces at work within our body/mind. For example, Difficulty at the Beginning, which is made up of the trigrams Thunder under Water, depicts the relationship between our sexual/emotional energy and our thinking process. Juggling these two powerful qualities is often experienced as Difficulty at the Beginning. When contemplating the hexagrams, it is useful to refer back to bodily correlates of the trigrams as anchoring points to help make the concepts more meaningful. Describing Difficulty at the Beginning as the work of balancing our head with our pelvis should help ground the meaning of the hexagram. Whenever the reader experiences difficulty in relating a particular hexagram to his or her own life, a moment's consideration of the bodily resonance involved will be very helpful in clarifying the meaning of the commentaries.

Facets of the Jewel

The trigrams are the essential alphabet of the I Ching. They are constellations of eight fundamental natural forces which interact to create the sixty-four hexagrams. It is the interaction between the trigrams which forms the basis of the imagery in the I Ching. The structure of the trigrams forms a basic sequence which is replayed at other levels within the book: one line above, one line below and one in the middle; Heaven, Earth and Human. The three lines describe a framework for the multitude of events in the natural world. As each line represents two possible states, The Creative or The Receptive, we have the permutations which form the eight basic trigrams.

For example, if the top line is yin (– –), or feminine, and the middle line is yang (——), or masculine, and the bottom line is also yang we have the trigram *Tui. Tui* has as its image a Lake and its attribute is Joyfulness. For the line of Heaven to be receptive and the lines of Human and Earth to be creative depicts a situation where the stability of human upon the Earth opens to the receptive guidance of the Heavens and thus Joy is abundant.
On the other hand, in the trigram *Sun, The Gentle Penetrating Wind*, we have The Creative in Heaven and in the position of Man, while the Earth is Receptive. The strength of The Creative in the two higher positions is brought into the Earth through its receptivity, hence the transition of energy is gentle.

This constant interaction of levels is crucial to the dynamic workings of the I Ching as a whole. In contemplating the trigrams it is important to remember that they are not static, but are dynamic interchanges of energy which, taken as a unit, depict fundamental patterns. Although they are represented by a simple solid or broken line, what actually is being suggested is a vital exchange of energy between different realms of being. The flow between The Creative and The Receptive across the warp of Heaven, Human, and Earth becomes a weaving depicting essential qualities of our lives.

The trigrams can be seen as crystals, faceted by the pattern of yin and yang, which focus our attention on particular areas of life. The light which passes through them is shaped by their form and given a certain hue, but it is free to continue on, entering other forms and changing once again. This is one of the secrets to using the I Ching effectively. Do not mistake the forms of the hexagrams for the answers; they are only the crystals through which the light of our awareness and insight are directed so that we can truly appreciate the movement of Chi or life force.

The following are contemplations of the trigrams and are intended to help orient the reader towards the eight fundamental energy systems of the I Ching. It is helpful for each individual to establish their own relationship to the trigrams so that in meditating upon them they begin to live... for when they become alive, then they can act as true guides for our journey.

The Creative, Heaven, Strength, Father

A blue sky that fills all directions, pregnant with sunlight, is alive with the potential of The Creative. The strength of Heaven is found in its vastness. Nothing has yet appeared upon the Earth and the spirit is free to move in unseen spirals. It may be that, as the thunderclouds of afternoon arrive, form will appear. Until then, life is held in a canopy of dancing blue.

When we contact The Creative in our lives we are filled with that sky. The spaciousness within us flows unchecked into all aspects of our daily world. Within this sky all the forms of our lives—jobs, relationships, aspirations, pains, fears, hopes, and sorrows—are free. The specific content of each may still be intact, but we are strong in our internal space and so can manifest creative impulses through and amongst them without resistance. The drama of our lives takes on a cloud-like quality: powerful, passionate, thundering, yet ephemeral, and we are always fundamentally aware that we are still in the sky, still in the seat of possibility and freedom.

The paradox of The Creative is that its emptiness is its strength. It is a strength born of wisdom: the knowledge of the seed. All forms are known first as an impulse of the unseen: the same one we feel when first inspired, first in love, first born; so full with possibility that we have the strength to begin the courageous journey of life.

The father, in this light, is seen as the underlying support of the family, not in form, but in inspiration and space. His masculine is not defined by his ability to control and dominate, but by his ability to live without attachment and without manipulation. Only with the quiet strength of the sky can the father really guide the growth of his family.

The Receptive, Earth, Devotion, Mother

The substance of the Earth is molded from within and without: deep tectonic forces betray the shifting of the very depths of the Earth's core. Mountains rise to give form to the surges below the surface. Canyons, rivers, plains and valleys are formed as the Earth touches the sky. Ever receptive, the Earth appears so solid, yet adapts itself endlessly to the currents which flow above and below.

To maintain such receptivity takes profound strength. Every mood, every emotion, every thought plays within our bodies, asking a new response and new expression from our form. The strength to give visible form to change is a stability which is born of an open and vulnerable heart, one that dares to touch the pain as well as the joy of life. To be Receptive we need a warrior's strength, unflinching in our stance yet never rigid. We must be able to receive all that life gives us and live our lives as a prayer of thankfulness. This prayer is a sacred posture which is a constant gift back to the
universe.

As we return what has been given we make room to receive once again. The Receptive is nurtured by consistent release... letting go again and again that we may receive again and again.

A mother's strength allows her to remain solid in the midst of incessant change. A baby bonds to the stability of the mother; if that solidity is contracted then fear is the legacy; if the solidity is dynamic, ever receptive, then the child is given the gift of renewal as its birthright.

Arousing, Thunder, Movement, The Eldest Son

Lightning flashes and Thunder rolls in its wake; creation is awake and moving. The urgency of creation breaks free in a surge of movement. This movement is meant to arouse, to awaken, to quicken.

The atmosphere just before a thunderstorm is thick, tense with expected change and darkened by the power which is gathering. Out of the darkness comes a light as electricity flashes to the ground: Heaven and Earth are once again in communion. The resolution of chaos is not easy and often demands the clarity and decisiveness of lightning-like action.

Thunder speaks to a time in our lives when movement is all-important. The stirring of our beginnings have become full-fledged action. When lightning is ready to strike, nothing stands in its way. This is a time when fear of change may appear as the face of our inner resistance. Understanding the inevitability of such movement, it becomes possible to surrender to its impulses. Carried into unexpected territory, we are able to remake our lives with a new respect for the power of creation. This respect is the inner attitude which tempers the development of our power and assures us of humility.

Keeping Still, The Mountain, The Youngest Son

A Mountain rests upon the Earth and remains firm as the seasons come and go. By virtue of its stillness, a Mountain remains secure through all the changes. Rising from the Earth, and yet part of the Earth, a Mountain is an altar which touches the Heavens, a sacred ground from which the heavens can be reached.

The I Ching was first formulated on the Siberian steppes of Asia. This high-mountain atmosphere was crystalline in its purity. Vast distances were telescoped by the clear refraction of light. The Heavens themselves were the threshold of this world.

Keeping Still has a quality of steadiness and forbearance which remains stable despite ever-changing moods and shifting life events. Internal strength, which maitains one's integrity no matter what the outer condition, is the Grace which the Mountain bestows. The capacity to remain steady in the discipline of one's life expression is one of the best ways to cultivate the qualities of the Mountain.

This is the trigram of meditation. The power of a mind which becomes still is such that even Mountains are moved. The central channel of the body becomes accessible when outer movement is released: this is symbolized by the structure of the trigram itself. The space between the two yin lines rises to meet the one yang line on top. This is mirrored in the rise of the spiritual fire in meditation. The capacity to hold a firm physical posture for long periods of time is a fundamental tool in meditation practice and is portrayed in the majesty of a Mountain resting on the Earth.

Keeping still can create inertia if one's inner attitude becomes rigid. Then the movement of life becomes something different than oneself and alienation and separation are the result. Pride, arrogance and judgment are indications of this fossilization at work.

The Gentle, Penetrating, Wind (Wood), The Eldest Daughter

Wind moves unseen across the Heavens and touches the four comers of the earth. The persistent effect of its actions scours canyons and carries dunes across the deserts. The rains depend on the unceasing work of the Wind. From hurricane to meadow breeze, the Wind embraces a full spectrum of moods and powers.

By virtue of its persistent action it is able to create great effect: this is emblematic of the power of penetration within our lives. If we remain faithful to a task, to a relationship, to a teaching, then we will, in time, uncover the hidden worth we seek.

The gentleness of the Wind and the Woods, is the gift of its persistence. By gentle application of will, over a long period of time, even the hardest of hearts are melted. A direct confrontation of force often only produces greater reaction and a hardening of boundaries.

The Wind is the breath of the planet and the movement of our own life force. Finding balance in our breath we can achieve steadiness of mind and penetrate to the essence of our hearts.

Our willingness to embrace the changes of life and the multitude of events and people in our daily world is supported by a heart which is receptive, yet strong. The Wind's strength is powerful, yet gentle enough to pollinate a flower. This application of force in a manner which can touch the heart is the benediction of the Wind.

The Clinging, Fire, Perception, Clarity, Dependence, The Middle Daughter

Fire clings to that which it burns. Light is created by the dissolving of forms. All of the visible world is bathed by light. This is a part of an eternal paradox; in order to see form, form itself must dissolve. The sun's gift is the warmth and light by which the world lives and yet the sun dies to produce this life. When a sun dies it gives off a last gesture of light. A supernova is one of the most powerful of celestial events. This gift of life is often seen as a guide—the biblical star of Bethlehem.

The clinging of light to the form it touches is a basis for perception. If photons did not interact with our eyes and cling to the molecules within, we would see nothing. If we do not consume what we see then have we really seen?

The Fire which burns between two hearts melts away separation and dissolves boundaries. This Fire consumes, and it can create great attachment. Unless we are willing to submit to the Fire of our relationships, then we will remain in the dark, whole areas of our being unexposed and unknown. The closeness of another strips away false pretense and leads to a true sense of oneself. This is a positive connotation of the Clinging. The Fire of relationship clings to those involved until they have become light. This means a burning away of egotism and self serving ways. What is left is the burning core of our spirits shining brightly as we radiate our common purpose.

21

The Joyous, Lake, Expression, The Youngest Daughter

A lake is held by the arms of the earth. Secure in such an embrace the lake can joyfully reflect the Heavens above. Looking upon a lake we see both the passing wonders of the sky and the mysteries of the Earth.

Only when we can relax in our own nature will our joy be free to fully express itself. The boundaries of a lake are firm and set clear limits. This is a strength which is necessary when forming relationships with others. Within clear and organic limits we thrive. Our expression then is pure and faithful, like a smooth surface of water awaiting the sky.

A lake is maintained by the flow of water which enters and leaves. Too much water and the resulting flood oversteps the boundaries and chaos is the result. Too little water and the Lake is sluggish with decay and is not vital enough to reflect clearly. Finding our balance between giving and receiving is the prerequisite to healthy expression.

Finding our balance within, we can reflect higher truth and merge our depths with the forms of the Heavens. This alchemy is forever changing, ephemeral, and most like a dancing lake's surface in its constant movement.

Light upon the lake becomes a scattering of pearls, each ripple catching the Fire which blazes above. Artistic expression which cultivates the qualities of the lake can wear the heavens like a finely woven garment. Each facet of our own gift reflects the light of a greater source.

The Abysmal, Water, Danger, Emotions, The Middle Son

Water flows always towards the deepest place: the hidden place, the place of submergence, that place in our lives where the unknown lurks. So much of our action is determined by the hidden forces which lie beneath the surface of our daily lives. Following the path of water we are taken into the hidden recesses and are apt to encounter the danger of the unknown, the danger of things long hidden. The journey into water is the journey into the depths of our souls... and that depth asks of us courage and the capacity to respond to the challenges of our lives.

Water is bound together by the mutual attraction of polarities in the molecules themselves; this simple fact allows all life on Earth to flourish. The fluidity of Water is symbolic of the cohesion when polar opposites unite through mutual attraction, and yet are not rigidly held nor mutually destructive. This becomes a model for right relationship with one another: bound together yet always fluid, ready to flow into the next situation without fear or trepidation.

Water is emblematic of our emotional nature. Emotions ebb and flow as the tides. Rising and falling, rising and falling, again and again. There is a danger in being swept away by the force of the movement. In working with the Watery aspect of ourselves, it is worth considering how Water flows. All Water in nature tends to gather into brooks, streams, rivers, lakes and oceans. It is helpful when dealing with deep emotions to have faith in the underlying matrix of our lives. This, in terms of our daily world, is the gift of our destiny: the overall pattern of our life purpose. In realizing this deeper level of being we can tolerate the tremendous power of our emotions as it flows through our lives.

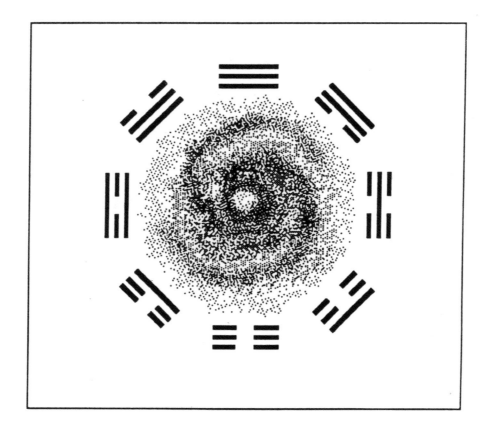

1

The Creative

The circulation of unconditioned energy forms the essence of the Heavens.
The Creative is persevering, of indomitable will,
and brings about movement without rest.
All things spring forth from the movements of the Heavens.
This is the essence of life, and its strength charges our lives with meaning.
The presence of Heaven invites the vessels of its expression to be known
as the substance of our lives.

The Creative is filled and yet empty.
As clouds spring forth from an empty sky,
so too, the Creative is teeming with life and purpose.

Will
Strength
Unending

The Creative

Heaven above: Creativity, Strength   Heaven below: Creativity, Strength

Light descends from the Heavens to become form: the image of The Creative. This initial spark of life is drawn from the unseen world of the Heavens and is the prime mover of creation.

The seamless curve of the sky is an invitation to reach outwards in search of the beginning. Looking past stars and planets which glow in the evening sky, we find an endless dance of solar systems and galaxies: an ever-widening array of spiraling light which is creation's song of becoming.

The Creative is an impulse which sustains the lover's touch and the course of planets; it is the inspiration of cathedrals, empires, and the currents of history unfolding. Touching this matrix of light (the weaving of the whole), we are sent with purpose and direction towards the fulfillment of our lives. The authority and conviction of the Heavens is an imperative which can lead us back to the stars themselves. These outer furnaces of transforming matter are but a mirror of the sustaining power of our core.

The still point of creation is a place of such power that we must circle around our center for many cycles before we gain the strength to make direct contact. Journeying around the mandala of the Self is the most sacred path we can walk. The hexagrams of the I Ching are way stations on this journey. They are stars of light in the passage of the night, each one a sun unto itself, and yet linked in a constellation which depicts the Tao itself.

We are that which we seek. The motive power of evolution springs forth eternally from The Creative and cascades down the corridors of time to fill each one of our lives. Our personal journey is empowered by an irresistible return to the fundamental ground out of which creation springs.

Our lives are the crucibles of The Creative. It is in each moment, in each action, in each thought, in each utterance, that we live out, and ultimately become, the all-pervading matrix of light and energy which sustains the universe. When Heaven descends to Earth, each moment is alive with light, and afire with the burning imperative of fulfilling destined expression. Linking ourselves to the power of The Creative, all of our actions, large or small, become radiant with self-sufficient power and grace. The song of creation is woven into the form of our lives. As we dance the dance of the Tao, we uncover the glowing bodies of stars within our hearts. These vortices of creative power are the moments of inspiration which infuse our lives with meaning and purpose.

Singing this song of creation, the I Ching begins...

The dragon seeks a place to land.
Ideas without form have no possibility of completion.
The Creative without the creation,
can this be the Tao?

Seeking, without resting, without receiving,
one cannot reach the goal.

Without the Earth can there be a sky?

Because what comes into being needs a form
The Receptive arises…

2

The Receptive

The Receptive awaits the movement of Heaven.
With quietness and serenity the Earth receives
the impulses of Heaven
and substance is given to the unseen.
The Receptive mind is still, yet moves with contact.
It gives form to endless impulses without being overwhelmed.
It never tires as it is guided faithfully by trust and surrender.

To cultivate such receptivity
we must have the courage to remain still
and trust that movement will arise as it should
and when it should.

Yielding
Devotion
Faith

The Receptive

Earth above: Devotion, Receptivity   Earth Below: Devotion, Receptivity

The womb of matter gives birth to The Creative. The Earth undergoes the labor pains of creation: for millions of years a mantle of matter gathers form and weaves the body of the Tao. The Earth has become a cradle of creation through unending devotion. Across the tides of time, the Earth has woven a constant response to the impulses of the spirit. This unceasing response is born of a profound devotion.

To be truly Receptive is to be remade continually by the heavens: a constant release of what has been generated. In order to undergo such a relentless process of change, firm foundations are important. Trusting implicitly in our own nature, we can surrender without reserve to the impulses of the Heavens. This trust is possible because we are, at the core, no different than the Tao. The paradox of this contact is that we are surrendering to our own being as we surrender to the power of The Creative.

The burning point of contact between The Creative and The Receptive is a dynamic moment of the potential becoming actual, spirit becoming form. Living our lives with such receptivity means being acutely alive with the power of creative action. All too often, people resist the deeply receptive places in their hearts because there is a fear of annihilation. If we are truly Receptive, then we are no longer in control; if we are no longer in control, then we fear we will be destroyed. This root fear is based on a mistrust of the Tao; for if we truly trusted, then we would unhesitatingly embrace The Creative and live our lives as expressions of the truth.

Closing deep upon itself, The Receptive forms a womb. This incubation is a spiraling inwards of intention and will. At the moment of purest intention, our will becomes the will of the Tao. There is a moment of intense receptivity just prior to the descent of inspiration. This fusion of personal will with the Tao is achieved by the discipline of our forms of expression. Artist, writer, dancer, poet, actress, and actor all cultivate the Receptive by virtue of their chosen discipline.

The Earth is heavy by virtue of its mass. An accumulation of matter builds a vortex of receptivity which is the nucleus of a planetary system. This gathering of form is necessary in order to sustain the fires of the creative process. In our own lives this accumulation of form is best done in a spirit of loving devotion. If we gather because of self-serving instinct and not because of faith, then we run the risk of materialism: cloaking ourselves with devices and material possessions to armor ourselves from the demands of The Creative.

A gathering of matter around the still point of the heart transforms our wombs into sanctuaries of love. For the love of creation we are willing to embrace our receptivity and honor the feminine…

In understanding the great work of joining
Heaven and Earth, we have
Difficulty at the Beginning...

3

Difficulty at the Beginning

The elements are mixed,
power seeks expression, and danger abounds;
This is a time of turbulence and upheaval.
The seeds of order are forged out of the turbulence of the times.
It is a time of discomfort,
but of tremendous promise.
Inner essence is covered by the swirling surface.
True growth awaits the revealing of that yet to come.
All manner of life is struggling to take form and become known.
In such times we should honor the turmoil
and have the wisdom to await its outcome. Beginnings are raw
with the energy of Thunder, fluid with the movement of Water,
and laden with the promise of new life. To cling prematurely to order
would be to violate the movement of nature.
Better to wait out the storm
and see what is born.

Electrical Energy
New Beginnings
Chaos

Difficulty at the Beginning

Water above: Danger, The Abysmal   Thunder below: Movement, The Arousing

Heaven and Earth have come into being, and in making contact, create Difficulty at the Beginning. The human realm is an intermediary between Heaven and Earth. It is the joy, sweat, pain, conflict, ecstasy, and work of our lives which bring the two together. This is not an easy task and is filled with confusion, chaos, and the turbulence of a thunderstorm. In the end, all storms come to resolution, and so it is in our lives; the rains will fall, the clouds will clear, the Heavens will once again be still, and the Earth will be nourished.

A difficulty inherent in any beginning is that the path ahead is not yet known. The masculine and feminine are in perpetual movement as they join in a dance of mutual understanding. The creative impulses of the Heavens seek the Earth for expression, and the Earth opens to give substance to new impulses. The changer and the changed are in a dynamic dance which is woven on the loom of creation and destruction. We long to quell the turbulence and assert a premature order so that we can once again be in control. The meeting of Heaven and Earth takes place at the root of our being, at the core of our structure. This arena is outside of time and space, and is beyond the control of our personalities. In order to bring in the new, we must be able to tolerate the turmoil of new beginnings.

Fearing difficulty, we often do not initiate new movement in our lives. The ability to appreciate the storm is the ability to embrace creative dissonance. Out of chaos emerges order, and if we are patient and allow the inherent wisdom of the situation to mature, the order will be a reflection of the Tao.

The inner fire of our true expression is often overshadowed during this time. The outer covering of our lives, the external personality, is seeking formation and looks, easily, to others for the mirror of its condition. This outer covering awaits the emergence of inner necessity in order that we may relax into what is.

A waterfall descends because it must. Gravity is the mother of its form. So too, at this time, seeking the river of our destiny is the guiding light for our actions. This discovery cannot be easily made by what we think, it is found by what our hearts are called forward to experience.

Clinging to clarity is inappropriate for this condition. The watery realms are flying in the Heavens and Thunder rolls in powerful surges. This is no time for analysis; it is a time for action, a time for creative leaps and devoted faith. Guided by the union of opposites, we are swept up by a grand alchemy. We would be foolish to think we could emerge unchanged.

Order and chaos hang in the balance of a new beginning…

Confusion and chaos
must be clarified
in the flow of life from the source.

This descent is brave
and at times foolish.
Because the young at heart
are able to make this journey
it is a time of
Youthful Folly...

4

Unknowing (Youthful Folly)

Water springs from within the Mountain,
rushing to fill unknown places.
There is an aspect of this flow
which is youthful and filled with folly.
The danger of advancing too quickly,
without examining the abyss we enter,
is that we may be carried
further than we reckon.
The courage to act must be tempered
by the stillness of the Mountain
in order to be fruitful.

Rapid Descent
The Fool
Courage

Unknowing (Youthful Folly)

Mountain above: Keeping Still   Water below: Danger, The Abyss

A spring which flows from under the Mountain cascades into the Abyss, abandoning itself to an unknown path. There is a certain grace which follows such action; a whole-hearted embrace of the experiences of life, even if dangerous, has its own protection. With the gift of innocence, a fool can go where the wise and heroic dare not tread.

Water is thorough in its capacity to fill even the darkest and most abysmal place. This ability to fluidly conform to all manner of surprises and dangers is the benediction of youth. Fear contracts the flow of life and interrupts our return to the source. As Water returns to the sea, so we return to our roots in search of meaning and understanding. Cultivating the fearlessness of a cascading river, we can fulfill the course of our lives.

This hexagram also points to the role of the teacher. In keeping still, we are able to guide young hearts without damaging their life force. Undue discipline and obstinate control weakens the will for learning and hinders the springs of inspiration. An overly sympathetic involvement in the drama of youth creates indulgence, and does not free them for their own journey. By cultivating the inner tranquility of the Mountain, we are able to influence others by our own example. Rivers flow from Mountains as they obey the laws of gravity. The structure of the Mountain itself helps determine the direction of their flow. There is no need for analysis or complexity, the river simply responds with innocence to the course of nature. Cultivating this quality of inner strength, we can effortlessly guide those around us.

Water which flows from the springs of the Earth is pure and vital. This vitality spills over to nourish the lands below. The initial stages of learning have a quality of inspiration to them which, if allowed full expression, can nourish us for years. The greatest of rivers, the arteries of continents, had their beginnings in Mountain springs. So too, the majestic movements of our life often have their beginnings in the folly of youth.

Honoring our beginnings means having compassion for the folly of youth. All too often our self-criticism erodes the passion of our life's expression. The courage to be ourselves means embracing danger and failure, as well as success and comfort.

A Fool's journey is sacred and may just return us home…

When the young begin their journey
they have need of nourishment.

They often rush eagerly past
the very places which could nourish them.
Wisdom is also found in Waiting...

5

Waiting

The Earth waits patiently for Water from the Heavens.
Resting in the faith that nourishment will come,
we can welcome the gifts which are given.
To grasp for nourishment prematurely
is to violate this trust.
Withdrawing our addictions, resisting manipulation,
we wait for the Waters from above.
Active with faith,
we turn reverently to the Heavens.
The expectation of Waiting
is the tension which builds faith.
Violating this tension out of fear
is to turn our back on the great mother
as She offers her gifts.

Nourishment
Patience
Trust

Waiting

Water above: Emotions, Danger   Heaven below: Strength, Creativity

Clouds which gather in the sky are harbingers of rain. The nourishment which the Earth awaits will come only when the Heavens no longer contain their Waters. Patiently we await the gift of the gathering clouds.

Often we grasp for nourishment and do not rely on our own inner strength. Building strength, we are able to drink deeply of the Heavens' nourishment and are not frightened by events. Implicit in this hexagram is the idea of drawing nourishment from difficult situations. If we wait for comfort and for security, then we may never find the nourishment we seek. The Earth does not question the Heavens about the coming storms. It simply waits and makes ready to receive what is given. If we prepare the ground for nourishment within ourselves, then we will have the receptivity to receive what is given.

In our relationships, we often complain that our partner is not giving enough. The impulse to give, to be generous, is a fundamental human attribute and is often deflected by our own inner attitude towards receiving. The ability to receive this gift is often injured by an early experience of loss. Rather than demanding nourishment, it is far better to till the soil and prepare to receive what comes. The complex interaction of two psyches is beyond the ability of our conscious minds to control, and we must surrender to the fact that often what is given comes from a realm that does not respond to personal demand. This rain from the Heavens is a descent of grace which cannot be manipulated or controlled by our own insecurity. In order to break the cycles of struggle which emerge in relationships, we must appeal to a more fundamental level of nourishment. Waiting for this realm to descend means strengthening our own faith and continuing our inner work.

Our expectations are all important in creating the condition for fulfillment. By studying the Heavens, by relating to the cycles of nature, we can gain a wisdom which will prepare us for true nourishment. Often what truly nourishes does not appear in pleasant circumstances. Recognizing true nourishment means to master the essence of Waiting. In the pattern of the Heavens, the unseen hand of the Tao stirs creation into being. This stirring is the ground of nourishment. If we can recognize this nourishment in our daily lives, then the simplest of gifts will nourish most completely.

Waiting, without expectation, we can welcome the Heavens…

40

Seeking nourishment and not finding what we seek
is the root of much conflict.
Searching for ourselves in others,
we lose sight
of their essence.

Losing their essence we treat them unkindly.
Treating them unkindly
we plant the seeds of discord.

In order to establish our boundaries
we engage in
Conflict…

6

Conflict

Heaven moves upwards and Water downwards:
the difference in tendencies brings Conflict.
Water is within, the dangerous rapids of unknowing,
and the strength of Heaven is above.
Strength supported by the hidden forces of our lives
can often lead to Conflict.
A thorough investigation of subconscious motives
will bring about resolution.
The rhythm of the waves reminds us of the patterns of life.
If we can understand Conflict as a rhythm of change
then we can come to peace amongst ourselves.

Self-determination
Boundaries
Rhythm

Conflict

Heaven above: Strength, Creativity   Water below: Emotions, Danger

The movement of Heaven is upwards and the movement of Water is downwards: the image of Conflict. Conflict results when a creative impulse leads in one direction and subconscious forces pull in a different direction. In attempting to integrate our creative inspirations with our past habits and tendencies, we may experience Conflict. Our impulse is to move in the direction of our inspiration, while our habits often appear to block that movement.

We often project our Conflict onto others. We find that which we should change in our own hearts in the actions of those around us, and demand that they change instead of ourselves. Implicit in the image of this hexagram is a suggested course of action. Just as ultimately the Waters of the Earth rise up to the Heavens, so too must we raise the unconscious forces within to the light of the Heavens. All Water on the Earth is moved by the moon (a heavenly body), and by becoming aware of the tides of change, we can resolve Conflict. What is below is guided by what is above: this is the image of resolution.

Often Conflict arises as self-assertion begins. Young children can be in open Conflict with their environment as they define their boundaries and begin to form a sense of self. Many of our Conflicts are a result of incomplete boundaries. We create Conflict in order to define ourselves. Perhaps by defining ourselves from within, we can demand less from our environment.

Pushing forward to resolve a Conflict is not always the best way out. Understanding the matrix out of which the Conflict arises often means adopting a point of view which is of the Heavens: the ability to creatively see the overall pattern and integrate the surging Waters of emotion into this vision.

Are the waves in conflict with the seashore or are they merely expressing the eternal movement of life? It all depends on the point of view held. Conflict is most often an indication of a divergence of energy. Understanding the needs of the moment helps honor our separate pathways. The reconciliation of our differences awaits our own internal clarification. Knowing ourselves first, we can then be with another in harmony.

Waves are made of the very same Water which lies still in the ocean depths. Is this not a hint as to how we can resolve Conflict?...

When Conflict arises there is a need to gather strength.
By building internal power
we can replace aggression with integrity
and decisive action.

Conflict asks us to seek
our foundations
and make them firm.

This is known as the Gathering of Force...

7

Gathering Force

Water gathers within the Earth;
strength flows within caverns.
We can establish healthy boundaries
and maintain them by being
strong within.
The Earth imbues its Waters
with The Receptive
so that when flowing
they remain sensitive and responsive.

Staying open, yet strong,
Gathering Force,
yet remaining mild,
we are assured of success.

Conservation
Containment
Force

45

Gathering of Force

Earth above: Receptivity, Devotion   Water below: Emotions, Danger

Water, gathering underground, creates aquifers which nourish the soil and replenish the land. This subterranean force is vital to the health of the land. The Oglala Aquifer, which covers a large part of the western United States, has watered the breadbasket of a continent. It is a resonant basin of Water which echoes the movement of life.

If power is stored within, then we have a vitality and strength which will protect us in our outer lives. Although cathartic emotional expression is occasionally valuable, it will leave the system weakened if it is prolonged. Just as dangerous is the subtle addiction to drama in order to give meaning and justification to our world. An impulsive expression of feelings leaves one vulnerable and often defenseless; however, the gradual gathering of feelings builds a strength which lends power and depth to their expression. Georgia O'Keeffe was an artist who gathered a force of expression which filled her canvasses with great power. Her home was simple and her emotional expression understated. She painted in an environment stripped of external comfort and color. From this inner austerity, she commanded great passion and expression in her art form.

A reservoir of feeling within allows us to be receptive and responsive to our world. Emotional exhaustion leads to inertia and insensitivity. The capacity to feel the world and its subtle undercurrents is the best defense in the face of danger. The Aikido Master has gathered this life force to such an extent that the aggression of an attacker has no place to enter; the force which approaches is returned with no apparent effort on the Master's part. We often armor ourselves against the pain of the world. The price we pay for such a defense is our inability to be truly receptive. By Gathering the Force of each event, whether it be painful or pleasurable, we build an internal strength which leaves our receptivity intact. Gathering Force, in this context, means letting each experience flow through us until it has reached completion. This completion of feelings builds emotional depth and creates a reservoir of strength.

Our depths filled, we have the force to remain true to ourselves…

Drawing from our own depths,
we are no longer dependent
and have the strength
to enter into
Union…

46

8

Union

Just as the Waters of the Earth
come together in streams, lakes, and oceans,
so we come together with others.
This is a force which we cannot resist
without violating our own core expression.
Resisting natural affinity will only weaken us.
The power of Union
will not be denied.

Attraction
Bonding
Destiny

Union

Water above: Emotions, Danger   **Earth below: Devotion, Receptivity**

Water upon the Earth coalesces naturally into lakes, streams, rivers and oceans. This spontaneous Union is the nature of Water and is a function of its very structure. The cohesive power of Water is what allows life on our planet to exist.

We so often resist the Unions which are inevitable to our own lives. Barricading ourselves with judgment and criticism, we resist an impulse which is as fundamental as the gathering rains. In recognizing this natural call to Union, so powerfully displayed by other mammals, we are asked to see the strength of our Union and to drink deeply of its nourishment. The wolves, dolphins, gazelles, and lions all bond in deep pools of union. Why do we think we are so different?

Water unites and yet each molecule remains intact and fluid. The surging tides, the raging whitewater rivers, and the placid lakes that reflect the changing colors of the seasons, all speak of the power of Union.

In uniting with others we need to be sensitive to the formation of our pools. Are we asked to initiate the call, or do we respond to a call already sung? Knowing when to join and when to invite others to join means that we must be sufficiently in touch with our own nature in order to gauge the proper direction of the movement. Once initiated, once the direction of the flow is determined, the Earth has little choice: the rivers cut into the ancient backbones of the continents. So, too, when we form a Union, we are inviting a flood of emotion, feeling, and sensitivity to flow. Our Unions should be strong enough to sustain the power of our emotions, and deep enough to guide the floods which occasionally wash through our lives.

We long for Unions and yet, once in them, often fight to be free. Union is the visible evidence of the inner movement of the Tao, and should be treated with respect and consideration. Once a Union occurs, the subtle matrix of the Tao is made manifest. The conditions which allow Union are determined not just by our desires and impulses, but by a response to a much deeper call, one which asks us to dance together in a celebration of life. Once embarked upon, the Unions should be carried to the final sea. The purpose of Union is to bring into action our heart's innermost impulses.

Like ripples in a Lake, our destinies overlap in Union…

When a Union matures,
a quiet discipline blossoms.

Living together,
we learn the necessity of inner conservation.

Attending to the details of our lives,
we build the foundation
of future expression
through the
Taming Power of the Small...

9

Taming Power of the Small

Wind blows in the Heavens;
unseen, yet moving.
A small change is the seed of future transformations.
Gently guiding our movement
is the power of love.

A clear Wind in the Heavens
is born of the sky,
yet caresses the Earth.

Such power is simple
yet profound.

Gentle Consideration
Attention
Detail

Taming Power of the Small

Wind above: Gentleness, Penetration   Heaven below: Strength, Creativity

Wind in the Heavens: the Taming Power of the Small. A gentle Wind blows, unseen across the vastness of Heaven. The Wind is an extension of Heaven, moving as the impulse of The Creative stirs and seeks expression.

Subtle shifts of sky precede a change in the weather. The entire force of The Creative is tamed by the simple movement of the Wind. This is a time for detailed examination of inner motives, an examination which should be gentle and thorough. Deep introspection, when linked with the force of The Creative, serves well. The crucial message of this hexagram is that self-examination must be linked with a larger vision of the universal creative cycles. If our self-analysis is not undertaken in this spirit, then we often become hypercritical and succumb to the paralysis of a too rigorous introspection.

An awareness of the power of The Creative allows us to prune away the small defects in our character and surrender to the challenge of a new life expression. Staying in touch with the small and simple tasks of the day is a gentle discipline which prepares the ground for greater challenges in the future.

Taming means to bring home that which is foreign to our nature. Often in the rush to find perfection and satisfaction in our lives, we lose touch with the daily rhythm of living. We become like strangers living in a strange land, and are alienated from our own homes. Embracing the Power of the Small returns us to the heart of our everyday world.

Attending to detail, we till the soil of future harvests…

In attending to the details of our lives,
we become aware of the importance of
each act during the day.

Proper Conduct is a pattern of action
which manifests truth
elegantly and directly
in our daily
world.

Realizing The Power of the Small
we give birth to proper
Conduct…

51

10

Treading (Conduct)

If one Treads on the tail of the tiger,
Beware!
Becoming aware of the effect we have on others
is the prerequisite of proper Conduct.

The boundaries of the shore limit the Waters
and give form to the Lake.
Observing our own boundaries,
we act with delicacy
and grace.

Such an attitude allows us
to slowly embrace the strength of the tiger.
This pace does not awaken aggression
and defensiveness.
By attending to our Conduct
we have the power to remake our lives.
This is the secret of Treading.

Proper Action
Diligence
Manners

Conduct (Treading)

Heaven above: Strength, Creativity   Lake below: Joy, Expression

If we Tread upon the tail of the tiger, then we need to be prepared for the result. Proper Conduct arises when we realize the danger of arousing the tiger. The tiger is symbolic of the instinctual primary forces of nature which, if not respected, can turn upon us and harm us. The tiger is also symbolic of autumn and the transition of light to dark.

Conduct in harmony with the Tao springs from a profound respect for the power of its ways. Proper Conduct is not an artificial imposition of rules designed to make us conform to an impossible ideal (the Victorian codes of etiquette). Rather it is an organic response to a recognition of the power of natural law. If you step on the tail of the tiger, you may very well be bitten. If we continue to pollute the planet and disregard the interrelatedness of nature, then the Earth itself will be doing the biting. The Hopis believe that the planet will be thrown off its axis completely if proper care of the Earth is not taken. The tiger is restless and grows angry with its abuse.

In the realm of relationships, proper Conduct is born of an understanding of the effect our actions have on one another. This understanding cannot be superficial. We must thoroughly examine the effect we have on others and respect the dignity of the tiger. Tendencies to blame and judge are often weak-hearted attempts to hide the clumsiness of our own actions. Continued abuse in relationships almost always returns as violent separation and difficult resolution. What bite the most are qualities which are lying deep in the waters of the Lake. Subterranean forces, formed by childhood hurts and difficulties, when stepped on tend to be expressed with aggression. These instinctual responses must be met with the strength and creative insight of the Heavens.

Conduct which is born of the Heavens is never mechanical and routine. It is endlessly creative in its solutions, and mediates the relative blindness of instinctual reactions. Conduct which reflects the Heavens is bound by the devotion of the Earth and nourished by the emotional fluidity of the Water. In this Lake the events which form above are clearly seen below.

The clouds, thunderstorms, stars and passage of the sun are all faithfully reflected on the Lake's surface. Our actions should reflect the Conduct of the Heavens if we are to be successful in life.

Cultivating moral strength, we touch the Heavens…

Proper Conduct assures meaningful boundaries.
Respecting one another,
we can live upon the Earth
in harmony.

Firm in our own actions,
we contribute to the flowering of
Heaven on Earth
and it is a time of
Peace…

11

Peace

Heaven supports the Earth
and the Earth expresses the Heavens.
Tranquility is attained
and longing is diminished.
Without longing, there is less desire,
with less desire, the mind becomes still,
and with a still mind,
we are nourished
by the fruits of creation.

Tranquility
Harmony
Balance

Peace

Earth above: Receptivity, Devotion   Heaven below: Strength, Creativity

The light of Heaven has descended and the warm embrace of the Earth has risen. Meeting, the two come to a point of balance, and Peace is the result. This tranquility is the fruit of our inner work. By elevating our mundane work and bringing down the highest ideals, we are able to release the tension of the search. So often, in our haste to transform and change, we sail past the goal and are carried into another cycle of frantic work. Peace arrives when Heaven is brought to Earth, and it is important to recognize the meeting when it happens.

Peace is not something which finally arrives after a long, difficult struggle (a kind of reward to be longed for); it is a quality which emerges whenever the two sides of our nature have come into balance. The more of Heaven we experience in our daily lives, the more Peace we experience. As our work proceeds, we are able to touch more and more of the tranquility which is our birthright. Resolution of opposites, the balancing of the masculine and feminine, is our greatest work.

When the light of Heaven shines brilliantly beneath the Earth, then illumination is complete. This tranquility is like a ripple spreading outward on a body of Water: gentle, but pervasive in its effect. All too often we struggle for Peace with such violence that we are condemned to be always grasping. By relaxing our defenses and allowing Heaven to enter Earth, we are responding to the urgency of evolution and can relax in the inner order of life.

Life is always unfolding, and if we can live with the impulse of The Creative surging from our own depths, then what is expressed is an organic blend of both Heaven and Earth. If we resist the creative urge of life, then we create tremendous tension which can become unrest, imbalance, and disease. Letting the very bones of the Earth ring with the illumination of Heaven means to imbue every action we take with the impulse of The Creative. The tranquility born of this inner alchemy is eternal and can never be taken from us, no matter how turbulent the outer world may seem.

Peace is the fruition of the descent of spirit into matter and the elevation of matter into spirit. This is indeed the great work.

Finding the Heavens in our daily actions, we are at Peace…

At the end of each breath
there is a pause before the next cycle of work.

In the space of this pause
all movement ceases
and the world is silent.

Within this silence
we are asked to plumb the depths of
Standstill…

12

Standstill

Heaven rises and the Earth falls below.
All action comes to a Standstill.

In such times it is wise to be still
and listen to the emptiness which arises.
Listening to the void
we may hear many things which cannot
be heard in the action of our daily world.

Having the faith to listen
without needing to act,
we are prepared for the
next cycle of becoming...

Turning Point
Pause
Void

Standstill

Heaven above: Strength, Creativity   Earth below: Receptivity, Devotion

Heaven rises and the Earth falls below: Standstill. The impulse to create and the substance which is created are no longer touching. This separation of Heaven from Earth brings the creative cycle to a Standstill.

The normal everyday world, where Heaven is above and the Earth is below, can all too often lead to a state of Standstill. The mundane cycles of existence lose their connection with the Heavens and inner stagnation is the result. If we are too complacent in relying simply on our everyday world, and do not undertake the great work of bringing Heaven to Earth, then we run the risk of losing touch with our creative ability.

In the void between Heaven and Earth, emptiness is found. Having the courage to plumb the depth of this emptiness is the key to transforming this situation. The void here is symbolic of the resting place between cycles, the gap between inhalation and exhalation, the moment when the pendulum changes direction. This void, though appearing empty, is actually pregnant with new possibility and potential energy. In our rush to fill this space, we distort the natural rhythm of life and plant the seeds of incomplete expression.

When we have the courage to plumb the void, to enter between Heaven and Earth, we are able to grasp the essence of being human. Our plight and our gift is to not be completely of either Heaven or Earth. We are made of both, and yet transcend both. By delving into the space between The Creative and The Receptive, we redeem the separation by sacrificing our pettiness and our limitations. By daring to encompass the entire realm of Heaven and Earth and contain the space between, we have distilled the essence of Standstill and are ready to move with authority and conviction. This movement cannot be self-willed, however. It must arise out of truly surrendering to the powerlessness of Standstill: nothing can move, nothing touches, nothing penetrates. Acknowledging this separation and remaining still is our only course of action. For in stillness we can become the totality of Heaven and Earth. In stillness we can touch the unknown where opposites are resolved, not through effort and will, but through an unfathomable act of the Tao.

In stillness we can touch the place between a man and a woman: the void which transcends sex and emotion and informs us of relationship. Often the struggle between men and women is the struggle to keep from standing still in the void. Only with the courage to face this inner void can we transcend the inherent differences between men and women and come to a realm of real relationship.

Entering the space between the worlds, we are shown many mysteries…

Standing still in the void,
alone,
a longing for companionship arises.

Stillness becomes movement
as hearts unite
in the Fire of Fellowship...

13

Fellowship

The light within our hearts
is the common bond
which forms our Fellowships.

The warmth of hearts uniting
blazes with a common purpose
and is the crucible of our communities.

Fire leaps into the Heavens;
clarity and strength unite.
The foundation of Fellowship
is found deep
within the heart.

Purpose
Service
Love

Fellowship

Heaven above: Strength, Creativity   Fire below: Clarity, Perception

A common Fire burning in our hearts unites us and leads us into action. A kinship based on mutual resonance establishes order and yet allows for fluid interaction. Clarity rises to meet Strength: this is the benediction of Fellowship.

The Fire of a common purpose unites divisive thoughts and establishes a harmony which transcends individual moods and weaknesses. Offering this action up to the Heavens, we join individual effort with the impulse of the Tao. When such a union is achieved, a Fire burns which is unquenchable.

The great religious movements of history are also examples of the power of this Fire. One idea and one belief emanating from the clarity of a great Sage unify countless differences and form enduring Fellowships.

Recognizing the light of our common purpose enables us to set aside prejudice and judgment. Guided by the strength of a common creative impulse we can organize forms which bring clarity and brilliance. The most successful businesses tend to form around a person of great vision and clarity. The Fire of an idea that is burning brightly is unquenchable.

The great innovators of history have dared to break free from the norm and see the world in a new way. In the spirit of this vision, Galileo dared to place the Heavens in perspective; Copernicus dared to envision the sun in its proper position; Newton dared to describe the mechanics of gravity; and Einstein plunged to the core of matter itself. When such fire burns it is because it is in accord with the truth. Each wave of change in science and technology arrives on the wings of a more fundamental understanding of reality. We are now living in a time when science is describing the world of the mystics and the mystics are describing the world of science. This convergence is the harbinger of a Fellowship which may be unlike any the world has yet experienced.

It is only when we are willing to describe the truth that our ideas and impulses have the power to heal and create true Fellowships. This beacon of truth is the great peacekeeper, for it kindles Fires of recognition in all parts of the world.

The Fire of our creative spirit is the guiding light of mankind…

In the common space of our hearts
great abundance is possible.
The rising current of love
fills the Heavens with Fire.

The flowering of our common
purpose is found
in Possession in Great Measure…

14

Possession in Great Measure

The Fire in the Heavens brings light to all the worlds.
Clarity, on the wings of strength,
infuses our daily tasks of renewal.
What has been started
is carried through to completion,
and the transformation
of our character is assured.
From the Fire of Great Possession
comes the strength
to undertake
our journeys.

Abundant Light
Fullness
Zenith

Possession in Great Measure

Fire above: Clarity, Perception   Heaven below: Strength, Ceativity

The sun has risen fully in the sky and at the height of its ascendancy it shines clearly over the Earth and illuminates the Heavens. Clarity has risen to a position of strength, and from this vantage point great things are possible.

When Fire burns directly in the Heavens, creative impulses are immediately transformed into light. This quality of illumination inspires, nourishes, and clarifies. When Fire is so clearly present, hidden places of inertia, doubt, and confusion are burned away. This is a time to offer up hidden motives and inner confusion to the radiance of the noonday sun.

When light is so predominant, great works can be attempted without fear of failure. The all-seeing clarity of the Fire in the Heavens will inspire and guide one's undertakings.

In such a time of abundance, it is best to cultivate modesty. The ascendant light is in accordance with destiny, and it is unwise to attribute such success to one's own efforts alone. The sun is a visible outer reminder of the inner flame which is traditionally depicted as the light of consciousness. This light renders the material world transparent; and when in touch with this light, the motives and workings of a myriad of beings are clearly perceived. This perception is sustained only by a magnificent gesture of the heart. To undergo the fire of spiritual transformation, one must be sustained by love. Matter itself is burned in the crucible of atomic power. The alchemy of the inner furnace is even more intense as matter is made transparent and all of creation shines with the same light of insight and awareness.

A light which shines in all directions has no preferences. There is neither high nor low, neither here nor there, neither male nor female, neither Earth nor Heaven. This liberating light is available in our relationships when we abandon judgment and return to the possibility of unsullied truth, then actions and events are no longer scrutinized under the distortion of preference. What appears is what is, and from that clarity we can see each other in truth. This is a Great Possession, and one which allows for a richness of spirit regardless of the outer conditions of the relationship.

The fire of the noonday sun guides all undertakings…

Filled with rising light
we must not fall prey to inflation.
In times of Great Possession
it is important to cultivate humility.

In humility we can temper
our power and move mountains
with our Modesty…

15

Modesty

The stillness and strength of the Mountain
yields to the Earth.
When our actions are blanketed by
The Receptive then we gain the strength of the Earth.
The humility to accept the circumstances of our lives
lends grace to our days.
If we resist our own becoming
then how can we move forward in life?

Wrapped in the arms of the Earth,
our pride is softened
and Modesty is in our hearts.

Humility
Embrace
Prayer

Modesty

Earth above: Devotion, Receptivity   **Mountain below: Stillness**

The strength of a Mountain rises clear and free from the surrounding landscape, and yet it is the Earth itself which folds to make the Mountain. This is the paradox of humility: the lowest is raised to the highest and the highest is tempered by the lowest.

A deep receptivity to life creates respect. Respect nourishes humility and strengthens our contact with the external world. Arrogance is most often born of fear, and fearful people are always creating towers of pride to cover their deepest insecurities. These insecurities are often created in childhood; the ways in which our parents were not present for us as children created wounds of abandonment which are waiting to be healed. How fitting it is that the Earth itself should be asked to heal these wounds. The Great Mother, the Earth, rises above the Mountain in this hexagram. The Mountain in this context is symbolic of our individuation, our separate selves. A mountain rises singularly above the Earth and is self-sufficient in its strength and grandeur. To bow in humility to the Earth is to acknowledge the debt we owe to our own mothers and to the mother Earth itself.

If we are modest in our approach to life, basing our impulses on respect and mutual support, then we do not over-step our position and create structures without true foundations. Reaching too quickly for life's rewards and not respecting the cyclical nature of growth, we erect skyscrapers of arrogance. With Modesty comes a tempering quality of steady growth and endurance.

The rich loam of the Earth is the fertile ground of future Mountain ranges. In time, the Mountains themselves will return to the estuaries and the meandering oxbows of the cultivated plains. Understanding this relationship, we cultivate humility and are assured of success in our undertakings.

In honoring our foundations, we become Modest...

When Mountains are humble
and power is worn next to a pure heart,
then what is conserved
leaps into expression
with Enthusiasm...

68

16

Enthusiasm

The Thunder of our life-song bursts forth
and is radiant upon the Earth.
Receptive to the movement of our lives,
we take risks and leap across
self-imposed barriers.
Carried by the strength of the Earth,
we have the energy to fulfill
the hidden currents of our destiny.

Breaking free of old perceptions
we climb upwards with the song bird
and the eagle.

Abandonment
Risk-taking
Energy

Enthusiasm

Thunder above: Movement   Earth below: Devotion, Receptivity

Thunder is the expression of movement which can no longer be restrained. The power of creation leaps into being, unchecked, and reverberates as a song of Enthusiasm. This is a movement born of the devotion of the Earth itself. Matter in devotion to its creator sustains the song of creation.

Emotions are powerful streams of feeling which, unchecked, can fall into confusion and depression. Enthusiasm, born of great devotion, forms a song of expression which can truly call forth the sacred. The uplifting and inspiring role of music helps to shape our emotions into a chalice for the sacred.

Being receptive to life, we are able to touch the pulse of creation. This heartbeat throbs in all manifest forms. Touching this pulse, we are invigorated and can enthusiastically join in the celebration of life. Expression born of devotion is a harmonious expression of the power of life itself.

Resisting excess, we must harness Enthusiasm to support our communication with one another. Too much joy and we are lost in our own intoxication; too little joy and our words cannot be heard. Finding the balance between the two, we are able to join together around the common thread of our humanity. Communication born of this receptivity is a melody which harmonizes and brings balance to our world. Singing is a way of bringing our hearts together and helping us to form stable social structures.

The Earth is the foundation which supports our Enthusiasm. Standing firmly on the Earth, in touch with our feminine, we are able to give impulse to The Creative. Such rootedness allows us to withstand the roll of Thunder through our lives. Such an awakening can be dangerous if we lose our ground and fall prey to inflation. Boundless Enthusiasm can drain our life force; we collapse into depression and exhaustion. Remembering the Earth, we can steer clear of wild mood swings and remain enthusiastic in the face of our life's work.

The song of life bursts from the Earth…

When Enthusiasm is present
the desire to learn
arises naturally,
like a flower opening to the sun.

In order to embrace new knowledge
we are called upon to Follow…

17

Following

The joyous Lake is stirred by Thunder.
Joyful movement allows us to change old habits
and be guided in a gentle manner.
Following a higher teaching
we are able to surrender to the currents of events
with joy in our hearts.
Resisting change, we dampen movement,
limiting movement, we extinguish joy,
losing joy, we have not the strength
to Follow.

Thunder awakens the depths of our expression,
stirring the unknown realms of inner Waters,
and calls forth new understanding.

Inspiration
Guidance
Learning

Following

Lake above: Joyous   Thunder below: Arousing, Movement

Thunder strikes deep into the heart of the Lake. Joy is set in motion by the arousing Thunder. Joyful movement is essential for being able to follow the pathways of life. Learning without joy is dry and empty.

This is the hexagram of the student. In following we are not enslaved, we are elevated. Without teachers in our lives, how is it possible to learn? Guidance must be slowly incorporated into our lives, or else it is mere authority and does not carry the weight of our convictions. The internalization of authority is essential if we are to walk free from resentment and domination. Paradoxically, in order to have our own authority, we must become students. Following a teacher with joy, we become supple and are able to grow without fear and anxiety.

The teacher is like lightning, striking quickly into darkness and the unknown, and illuminating the hidden places in our lives. This illumination stirs the innate joy within us. Once moving with life, we are able to feel the joy of creation. Joyful in our expression, we are able to follow more deeply into the sublime and mysterious realms of life. The very depths of the Lake invite us and await our movement.

The dolphins in the sea follow one another with ecstatic rhythm. The lead dolphin is so much in harmony with the rest that it does not appear to even be a leader. The startling illumination of a teacher's insight, when coming from a true teacher, feels like the whisperings of our own souls. A true teacher's knowledge is not something foreign to us, it is more a feeling of coming home.

We should celebrate this period of learning, and rejoice in our capacity to follow. Our depths have been stirred, and we are once again in touch with the wellsprings of life. When our depths are stirred the unknown is often made visible. In the absence of a teacher this can be frightening. The authority of a lightning strike is such that even the most subconscious quality is shaken into movement. This ability to move the resistant and repressed qualities in our lives is the true function of a teacher.

Remember, the teacher is that which teaches and can be as simple as the spring wind, or as complex as an entire society. The power of the teacher is really only possible when we are able to follow, and in Following we are able to joyfully celebrate life.

True guidance stirs inner joy…

Following mature guidance
we are made aware of what is true
and what is false.
Working on the false
to uncover the true
leads us to the doorway of Decay…

18

Decay

The gentle Wind cannot move the inertia
of the Mountain
and stagnation is the result.
This is a time when our inner decisions
have taken us out of the external flow,
and Decay sets in.
The work required in a time of Decay is to foster
movement and attention,
and resist indifference and apathy.
Consistent work will bring forth its own renewal.
We must not lose heart
in the undertaking.
The seeds of the spring are nurtured
by the Decay of autumn.
Life is given new substance by the passage of the old.

Assessment
Attention
Focus

Decay

Mountain above: Stillness Wind below: Gentleness, Penetration

Wind gathers at the base of the Mountain and falls back upon itself, unable to sway the inertia it faces. There is a fundamental split between the gentleness of the Wind and the stillness of the Mountain. When not in harmony these bring about a Decay of life force. In a period of Decay, we must cultivate awareness and movement as antidotes to passivity and inertia.

In many parts of the world there are disturbing Winds which blow seasonally: the Santa Ana, the Chinook, the Foehn. When these Winds blow, the population is irritable and unsettled; mental illness rises and there is a quality of unrest in the air. These Winds demonstrate the principle of Decay. The Winds are associated with major Mountain ranges and the pressure differential which builds up atmospherically as a result of the uplift in the land. Negotiating the form of the Mountains, the Wind is compressed and driven to the low lands, often with destructive results. Too much movement, when at odds with the landscape, produces Decay. We would expect movement to be positive, but when thrown out of balance with its environment, it is destructive.

Implicit in the inertia of the Mountain is a hint as to how to re-direct the energy of our hearts, the breath of our life. By quieting ourselves, yet avoiding stagnation, we touch the true nature of our inner landscape; our breath flows in harmony and we can begin a period of renewal.

Work that is in relation to the world around us brings the discipline necessary to move Mountains, if need be. Too often we take on work for reasons of greed, fear, or despair. The fruit of this work is Decay, for we have not felt the true landscape and have distorted our world view with false impressions. Work that is in harmony with the natural order frees us from the conditions of Decay.

A loss of heart in our work leads to inner Decay. The impulse for gentle movement is blocked and we fall into stagnation. Work which is founded on joy leads to the gentle penetration of the spirit in our lives. This is the challenge of Decay: to transform our inner relationship to the world around us so that our work is fruitful and in balance.

The seeds of true work are often found in the most stagnant of places…

76

Taking upon ourselves the work of real change,
we orient our lives towards
possible greatness.

Often the darkest hour is necessary
to redirect our attention.
Inspired by renewed determination,
we experience a revolution in our Approach…

19

Approach

Aligned with distant majesty
we cultivate the ability
to integrate higher principles into our lives.

In Approaching something great we must be steady.
The Lake lies secure in the arms of the Earth
and is able to reflect the Heavens.
The attitude we adopt
often is the strongest guide
as we walk upon our path.

Seeing the highest,
we plant our feet accordingly.

Point of View
Orientation
Attitude

Approach

Earth above: Devotion, Receptivity   Lake below: Joy

The Chinese word "lin," translated as "approach," also has a traditional meaning of "becoming great." The Approach we adopt in life is often what makes the difference between mediocrity and greatness. There was a period in Gandhi's life when he was very tentative, and could have easily lived his life in the obscurity of practicing law and raising a family. He forged his purpose when he approached the world he lived in with a burning sense of justice. His Approach became one of uncompromising steadfastness in the face of injustice. This inner attitude matured until it changed the course of history.

How we choose to Approach a situation is often what determines the eventual effect it will have in our lives. There are many events which are beyond our control, and our only real power lies in the Approach we take in relation to them. Becoming great, in this context, means to Approach life with the readiness to draw forth inner power and clarity, even in the face of adversity.

Having become great, there is then the added difficulty of how to Approach others. The unwavering devotion of the Earth and the inexhaustible depth of the Lake are linked to give the gift of this greatness back to the world. Devotion, humility and joy are qualities associated with truly great individuals. This is a clue as to how to support the strengths within each one of us. In our strengths we find the support of the Earth and the joy of the Lake, and give them readily to those around us, for only in truly sharing our strength with others is that strength ever made complete. Proper Approach towards those around us assures us of a deepening of our hearts. The Earth, which holds the Lake, supports without compromise. When we are unselfish in our support, we can Approach others in a manner which builds the inherent greatness in every soul.

Approaching the center, we become great; becoming great, we give; in giving, all of life finds order. The tenderness of our Devotion assures us of a proper attitude towards the unseen workings of the Tao. Having formed such a relationship, we are assured of success.

Our attitudes form the path which takes us to the furthest peak…

Having steadied our Approach
we are now fit
to view the world with
hearts of equanimity
and minds as spacious
as the sky.
To view the world clearly
is to enter into Contemplation...

20

Contemplation

The Wind blows across the four corners of the Earth,
steadily gaining wisdom
as it flows across the landscape of Creation.
Cosmic order is embedded in the natural world
awaiting our Contemplation.
Contemplating the order of nature,
we can come into harmony
with truth and rest in the wisdom
of the Tao.

Hidden Order
Pattern
Matrix

Contemplation

Wind above: Gentleness, Penetration   Earth below: Devotion, Receptivity

The Winds which blow across the Earth are free to see the greater patterns of nature. Mountains, rivers, and valleys are ripples on the surface of a cosmic dance. Frozen in geologic time, the footprints of creation itself are unmistakable.

Contemplating nature takes us inward and informs us of a more profound order, one which is subtle and all-pervasive. Just as the Wind penetrates all places in the Heavens, so pure Contemplation makes us wise.

This wisdom is born of freedom. It is only in the Wind's freedom that wisdom is able to range far and see the rising and falling of events. Consider the balance of our breath with our heart: two rhythms which synchronize continually to bring us life. The heartbeat of the Earth, joined with the rise and fall of the Winds, forms the body of our planet. There are caves in the Four Corners area of the United States which breathe with a regular cycle of inflowing and outflowing air. In becoming sensitive to these greater movements, we are able to strike a pose of balance and Contemplation.

Contemplation is a steadying of our minds. From such steadiness we can touch the hidden pathway of the Tao. The mind which searches for the hidden meaning of life disturbs that meaning with its very search. The mind which gently flows across the pattern of Wind and Earth is taken to the heart of meaning and rests there naturally.

Can we contemplate each other in the way we contemplate the Earth? Without reacting, withdrawing, or manipulating, can we simply follow the breath of our movement together and be taken to the wellspring of truth which awaits our discovery? Contemplation is a temple of respect: a gentle, yet penetrating, awareness which fosters true humility and a Sage's sense of destiny in the daily workings of our lives.

In Contemplating the natural world, we are given its hidden secrets…

Contemplating the world,
we are guided into action
by the manifold grace of Creation.
This action is the foundation of
Biting Through…

21

Biting Through

The movement of Thunder joins the clarity of Fire
producing emphatic action.
Clarity without movement
can be ineffective,
movement without clarity
can be dangerous.

Vision and action in balance
produces clear results in the world.
The decisiveness of the times
eliminates doubt and
fosters strength.

Lightning-like in our clarity
we achieve justice
in difficult times.

Decisiveness
Resolve
Action

Biting Through

Fire above: Clarity, Clinging   Thunder below: Movement, Arousing

Out of the clarity of Fire, Thunder emerges; action born of insight cuts to the heart of any obstacle. Biting Through is a call to resolute action. The slash of a sword dispels illusion and clears the pathway to courageous action. Lightning does not hesitate before striking, Fire does not hold back once lit.

The tension of opposites is resolved in a single stroke of action. In the face of an obstacle we often contract and hope to study the situation in order to control the events we are afraid of facing. Biting Through speaks to a powerful and direct approach which surrenders our hesitation to the imperative of action. This is a resolution which is born of courage. It takes great courage to act, and yet, in acting, courage is given.

Clarity without action can be immobilizing, and can weaken us through its very strength. Action without clarity can be numbing, and can trap us in events which inexorably bind our freedom. Like a sword's edge, polished and tempered to perfection, the balance of clarity and action frees us from bondage to the past and opens the way to new life.

The balance of justice is often tipped by a prolonged period of struggle. In rectifying the situation, a lightning-like release is needed. Often, the accumulated tension of a long period of dispute creates a charge which can only be released in a thunderous display in the Heavens. The awe-inspiring quality of a major electrical storm helps cultivate a sense of humility in the face of inexorable forces. This humility, when coupled with decisive action, gave Gandhi the power to cut India free from British domination: a living embodiment of Biting Through.

Resolute action is the threshold of freedom…

Decisive action must be balanced
by a gentle appreciation
of the beauty in the world.

Honoring the perfection
of the Tao we open
the doors to Grace…

22

Grace

Fire plays upon the Mountain;
dancing light upon the facets of the jewel.
The elegance of nature
inspires deeper reflection and concentration.
The purpose of aesthetic beauty is to foster
a more profound contemplation
of universal order.

Inspired by the beauty before us
we are led to contemplate
the beauty within.
Grace opens the gateway
to a more thorough investigation
of our lives.

Aesthetics
Inspiration
Beauty

Grace

Mountain above: Keeping Still   Fire below: Perception, Clarity

Beauty is the handmaiden to the soul. In contemplating beauty, we are taken to the doorway of our own inner self. A Fire that burns beneath the Mountain illumines the cliffs with dancing light. Light clings to that which it shines upon: this is the secret of Fire. The luster of creation is the adornment of the Tao.

All manner of beauty is material for the flames of appreciation and clarity. Our perception, resting on any object, becomes a burning gateway to more fundamental realms only if we can cultivate the stillness of the Mountain. Without inner calm, we do not have the steadiness to appreciate the subtle. Without appreciation of the subtle, we cannot live easily in a world of difficulties and trials.

Grace between two people means a Fire of love is burning. The heart's Fire spreads light across the stillness within, and inspires us to continue our journey together. Deep within, there is a quiet which is the threshold of the soul. Without the light of love, that stillness is often frightening, for it can feel very impersonal, even alien at times. The heart's Fire burns by consuming fear, doubt and separation. The light of this Fire strikes deep into the darkness, and gives us the strength to continue our journey inward. There is a saying in China that the nature of humankind is found in the center where emotions are not yet manifest. Grace takes us to the threshold of this center.

Appearances are the cloak of creation, and should not be mistaken for the essential movement of the Tao. The Grace of exterior beauty is a Fire which can blind as well as open. By cultivating the stillness of the Mountain, we can stay firm and not be confused or distracted by the sheen of the everyday world. Walking through the world of appearances is a fine balancing act: cultivating an appreciation for the beauty of manifest creation, yet remaining able to penetrate to the heart of the unmanifest.

Clarity and stillness are the benediction of artistic expression. These are the gateways to a more serious investigation of the Tao. Inspired by the beauty around us, we are able to continue the journey with Grace and tranquility...

If we become entranced in external beauty,
then our foundations dissolve
and we can no longer remain firm.

Without an adequate foundation
we are subject to Splitting Apart…

23

Splitting Apart

When unnecessary structures in our lives
fall away,
new movement emerges.
The stillness of the Mountain
and the humility of the Earth
point to the correct attitude
in a time of Splitting Apart.

Quietly understanding
our transformation,
we are ready to continue our life's work
in spite of the apparent collapse
of our world.

Transformation
Falling Away
The Essential

Splitting Apart

Mountain above: Keeping Still   Earth Below: Devotion, Receptivity

In this hexagram, five dark lines rise and dissolve the final line of light. When the forces of the unconscious rise there is often a fracturing of our daily world. The ground beneath us heaves with the emergence of unseen matters, and our outer structures can no longer remain the same.

This can be a frightening and alarming time, particularly if we cling to the last vestiges of our old ways. The upwelling of darkness is a necessary event and cannot be avoided. The cycles of change which determine the world all have a component of darkness. If we struggle to hold onto our old beliefs and conditions, then the darkness is feared as an evil. If we recognize the eternal dance of light and shadow, then we can enter the darkness knowing that it is an initiation which will ultimately strengthen us and make us whole. This does not mean giving in to inferior forces, rather, it is the hero or heroine's journey into the underworld so that we can know the totality of life.

Inner stillness and humility are the qualities which are helpful on this journey. Pride breeds restlessness and is always seeking to prove itself. Such agitation leads us to identify with the content of our inner darkness and fall prey to negativity. Only a still and stable mind can look fully into the darkness and see the light beyond. A mind which is restless will become lost along the way, for it does not have the inner conviction to complete the journey.

Splitting Apart means allowing the old to collapse so that the new can be born. The earliest whispers of birth can often feel like death. We know something is about to change, but have not yet realized the moment of conception. This period before conception is often the darkest, for our life energy begins to recede and we do not even realize the cause. A willingness to allow collapse is born of faith in the universal process. The tides retreat because they will advance; breath exhales because it will enter again; leaves fall and decay so that new ones may appear.

Humility arises in recognizing the source of life's cycles. Arrogance is believing that we have control when, in fact, we are really engaged in desperate attempts to stave off an inevitable surrender to the mysteries of the Tao. Stillness is the gift of true perception. Seeing into the nature of life, our hearts are steadied in the face of advance and decline.

The old falls away so that the new can emerge…

The husk has fallen away.
The seed of new light
is once again present.

The old retreats
and the new Returns...

24

Return

The Return of light after a period of darkness.
Light emerges
and the seeds of new growth
have been planted.

New hope is like a whisper in the winter's winds.
Spring is felt
and yet not clearly seen.
New beginnings are emerging
from the mantle of the Earth.

Understanding the inevitable changes of life,
we accept our cycles of growth
with devotion.

New Beginnings
Winter Solstice
Seeds of Light

Return

Earth above: Devotion, Receptivity   Thunder below: Movement, The Arousing

Light enters at the nadir of darkness: another cycle has come full circle. Thunder resounds below the mantles of the Earth; there is a stirring to return to the Heavens, to return once again to the spacious skies where thoughts dissolve into the purity of a still mind.

The Earth trembles with tendrils of new light. This is the time of the winter solstice. The stirrings of a new year are felt, and it is a time to harmonize our lives with this movement.

Timing is all-important. If we catch the wave of the new year, then we can return with the light, and old habits and faults fall away like the spent leaves of autumn. If we miss that moment, if we fail to rest as the light begins anew, then we run the risk of working against the very force which seeks to aid us.

A Return to great ideas, to lofty thoughts, to a contemplation of spiritual truth is called for. The seeds we plant with the new light will be germinated with the coming of the year. This is a time to put aside false pride and inner aggression, and join in a renewal that is cosmically determined. The Earth turns once again towards the sun, and this is the benediction of the planetary dance. We must fall into step with a rhythm that is far greater than our petty concerns and idle worries.

Light journeys underground in order to redeem the darkness. The Thunder of our souls is a sound which must be heeded if we are to transform the leaden cloaks of doubt and unease. Far better to wear a mantle of devotion than one of confusion. The insulation of a devoted heart is such that the seeds of light are grown to full maturity.

Between friends, a Return means to remember the essential bond which brought us together in the first place. Returning to the heart of our friendship, we reawaken the fruit of our union. Joining together in answer to the Thunder's call, we cull the best of the previous cycle and prepare our soil for new and unexpected growth.

The Return of light is an answer to our prayers, a response to the whisper of longing that we have carried deep within. When that which we have longed for is finally glimpsed, then our longing quickens and gives us strength for the coming year.

New light leads us into the new cycle…

Returning light
is free of guilt,
free of old conditioning,
and carries in its wake
the gift of Innocence...

25

Innocence

Thunder quickens the new growth of spring.
Unexpected growth emerges
from the teeming life force
of the Earth.
The Heavens are resounding with new beginnings
and Innocence is all-pervasive.

Acting without ulterior motive
we follow the path of life
and we return
to a fundamental energy,
a pristine expression
of creativity.

Unexpected
Unconditioned
Pristine

Innocence

Heaven above: Creativity, Strength   Thunder below: Movement, The Arousing

In the spring of the year Heaven manifests on Earth as the Thunder of new growth. Everywhere new life quickens and emerges. The will of Heaven is unsullied and erupts spontaneously. The spontaneity of an innocent mind assures us that the will of Heaven will flow effortlessly. Self-serving attitudes, based on the desire for personal reward, strip away Innocence and block the natural descent of Heaven.

At our core is a gift of purity which is the heartbeat of the Tao. This unsullied essence is stirred by the Heavens themselves. It takes Innocence to touch this gift without distorting its true nature. An innocent mind sparkles with fresh impulses of the Tao: the dance of light on new powder snow, a mantle of Innocence upon the land. A mind of snow-white purity acts with the inner authority of Heaven and is unceasingly free. Not bound by convention, unconscious habit, or expectation, the Innocent is a true child of the spirit.

The Thunder of the Earth as it responds to the Heavens is the song of spring: green leaves budding and new forms bursting into patterns of flowers, streams, and woodlands. This is an ecstatic dance: an embrace of the arousing. Embracing Thunder, we cannot hang onto old ways; we are reborn in Innocence and swept clean by the power of new life.

Endless self-reflection and analysis can sentence us to the prison of patterns long worn out. Being open to the unexpected can dissolve long-standing prejudice and judgment, and set our child free to dance once more. Instead of striving to protect ourselves in our relationships, always looking for ways to be safe, we let the unexpected wash us free of our limitations.

The innocent mind is a strong mind, filled with life-force and bursting with new expression. No time for fear, no space for fear, only the fullness of The Arousing fulfilling our hidden destinies. This is the legacy of the Innocent: to be gift bearers of the sacred and bring change to the world of form.

Inner purity blossoms upon the wings of Innocence…

Innocence is able to warm
the heart of the most powerful.

The Heavens stir within the Mountain
and creative energy
is given form.

With purity
we are able to
Tame the Power of the Great...

26

Taming Power of the Great

In stillness we can gather
the vastness of Heaven
and give it form.
This is a time of storing power,
limiting outside action
and gathering inner strength.
Acting prematurely
will limit possible expression
by dissipating
power prematurely.

The Mountain tames
the fullness of the Heavens
with the serenity
of its stillness.

Containment
Inner Strength
Building

Taming Power of the Great

Mountain above: Stillness   Heaven below: Creativity, Strength

Heaven within the Mountain: this is the Taming Power of the Great. Inner stillness, when cultivated regularly, can take us to the Heavens. The strength of the Heavens is tamed by the stillness of the Mountains. This speaks to the heart of the creative process. If we are to give form to the impulses of Heaven, then we must quiet ourselves through discipline and attention. The impulses of The Creative are very powerful and must be tamed in order to come into being. Our own quiet, in mind and body, provides the necessary mechanism to touch The Creative directly.

This is the hexagram of study. By contemplating the truth of those who have gone before, we are led to the gateway of our own expression. In such study we are prepared for our own contact with the source of creative inspiration. A prolonged course of study in any discipline begins to train the student in the way of the Tao. The laws of life are the same whether it is engineering or ancient history. By a consistent application of will to the chosen field of study, a student is made fit to make their own creative contact. If the Heavens are not tamed properly, then the storms which sometimes rise may uproot our daily lives and push us to the edge of insanity. Carl Jung was able to maintain many years of direct confrontation with the unconscious by virtue of his discipline as a scholar and his service as a healer; whereas Vincent Van Gogh, despite his artistic achievements and contributions, was pushed over the edge by a similar contact with the numinous source of Creativity.

Daily renewal of character is made possible by a combination of strength and firmness. The eventual source of strength is the creative urgency of the Tao. Creation does not end with the birth of forms; the energy of the act transcends time and is continually flowing through every moment of our lives. This is a subtle strength which, if accessed directly through meditation (Keeping Still), will enable us to have success in many aspects of our lives.

We have the possibility of being reborn each day if we can reconnect to the original impulse of creation. Only the Mountain peaks have the silence necessary to remember such an event. The yogis of India and the medicine people of the Native traditions in the New World both journeyed to the Mountains in order to contemplate the divine. The pulse of creation is most easily felt when Mountains lie beneath our feet.

The Heavens gathered within prepare us for the Fire of expression…

When power is contained
and boundaries are made clear,
then it becomes clear
as to what is within and what is without.

Knowing clearly this distinction,
real Nourishment is possible...

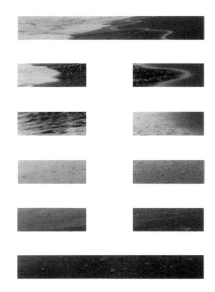

27

Corners of the Mouth (Nourishment)

Thunder in the Mountains
strikes close to the heart
and wakes us from illusion.
Seeing clearly the distinctions between
ourselves and others
is the threshold of Nourishment.

Shaken from self-concern
by the immediacy of our contact
we are able to receive
what is given.

Movement above
and stillness below
form the gateway
of assimilation.

Assimilation
Nourishment
Balance

Corners of the Mouth (Nourishment)

Mountain above: Stillness   Thunder below: Movement, The Arousing

In order to be properly nourished we need a balance between action and rest: too much movement and we cannot assimilate what is given. Our minds are always leaping ahead and never resting in the moment. Such speed creates a hunger which is difficult to fill. In being too quiet we lose the Fire necessary to digest what is given. A balance between the two assures us of our proper Nourishment.

There is a void in many lives which is the source of many addictions. This void is a symptom of a lack of harmony between action and rest. Always seeking movement, we are endlessly empty because there is no space created to receive. Resting too long, the blur of life in motion becomes a source of fear and we become separated from the Tao. This void is only an illusion emanating from the missing half of our experience. To try to fill the void with external objects defeats our actions. It can only be filled by finding the missing quality, be it Thunder or the Mountain.

Thunder moves around the Mountain. The peaks remain still as lightning shatters the alpine quiet. Running in fear of the movement will cripple us; resting too long on the edge of the abyss will immobilize us. It is only when the stillness of the Mountain becomes the fulcrum of our motion that we have the balance necessary to receive Nourishment.

In order to nourish one another, we must find tranquility in the dance which arises as two beings learn the subtle art of blending yet standing alone. We often create confusion by demanding movement because we are afraid of stillness, and we insist on stability when what we need to do is move. If we can see the Thunder in another's eyes, yet feel the tranquility of their heart, we will be able to nourish them and be nourished ourselves.

Thunder dispels the tension of prolonged quiet. A calm evening, when the Mountain sky is wrapped in sunset colors, brings peace to a heart left shaken by the storms. Nourishment comes when Thunder stirs and Mountains rest within our hearts.

In the balance of action and rest, we find true Nourishment…

Taking Nourishment we are filled,
and in fullness
comes the need for movement.

Movement which follows Nourishment
can often feel like
The Preponderance of the Great...

28

Preponderance of the Great

Inner movement rises,
the Wind stirs the Lake from within,
the call of our hearts
breaks against
the confines
of our limited expression.

This is a flood of energy
asking for
new worlds
and new actions.

Old anchors no longer work,
new foundations
must be built
to secure this excess.

Imperative
Movement
Excess

Preponderance of the Great

Lake above: Joy   Wind below: Gentleness, Penetration

When a ridgepole is not secured, and the weight in the middle exceeds the proper support, there is a danger of collapse. Accumulating too much energy at the center without enough grounding can be very dangerous. Vincent Van Gogh painted with a passion that captured light itself, and yet, in the end, he was unable to maintain his balance and succumbed to the forces which he had summoned.

This hexagram presents a hint as to how to remain grounded when the floods descend. Gently penetrating to the fundamentals of life and balancing the terror of the cyclone with the joy of simple action can help maintain balance. The tree which is rooted in the Earth may bend in the torrent of Water, but it can recover its poise because of the simplicity of its foundation. The depth of its roots have sunk low into the Earth in search of moisture. When Water oversteps its bounds and appears as a flood, the tree survives because it has diligently searched for the source of its nourishment.

If we seek daily for our source, then we build the strength to withstand contact with our core when it finally arrives. We carry within the power of literally being able to create and sustain worlds of differing experiences. This creative potential, when tapped directly, can be overwhelming if we have not conditioned ourselves for the contact. This is one of the secrets of spiritual practice.

The preponderance of masculine energy in the core is asking to be recognized. Often we feel as if we are about to be torn free from our moorings as we come into contact with our inner masculine. The force of manifestation can create chaos as well as beauty.

Our relationships provide the crucible in which we can bring the masculine and feminine into balance. These times of intense inner opening can be trying on our outer relationships if we have not done our homework. Attending daily to all of our relationships and examining our actions with incisive compassion will help build the foundations necessary to withstand trying times.

With foundations of love and joy, we withstand the flood...

When energy descends
to become torrents
of cascading
movement,
we are taken to the depths of Water...

29

The Abysmal (Water)

Water, which flows relentlessly towards its goal,
fills all crevices
without fear or regard for danger.

Remaining faithful to its own nature
it moves forward
under all situations.
Water, in constant movement,
will eventually
bring to surface
the most hidden of conditions.

The flow of our lives
should be constant
and without fear,
like the Water returning to its source.

Continuity
Return
Flow

The Abysmal (Water)

Water above: Danger, The Abyss   Water below: Danger, The Abyss

Water flows without fear back to its source. Though dangerous chasms and hidden canyons may deflect its course, eventually it returns to the sea. Our emotional life flows continually towards its source. If we forget this and become lost in the eddies and torrents along the way, then our emotions obscure our journey. If we remain true to our essential flow, then the drama of our life becomes the vehicle of its own transformation. Whirlpools, undertows, riptides and cataracts all resolve themselves eventually in the greater movement of life's Waters.

Hidden tendencies and old pains tend to settle in the deepest Waters of our being. If we do not have the courage to dive into these hidden currents, then we run the risk of losing vital sources of energy. Streams and rivers fill the most hidden areas of the Earth. They flow into such depths because they have no choice. They are impelled by gravity to seek the lowest possible resting place. Likewise, we often must enter dangerous areas in our own psyche if we are to return to our source.

Water is the medium which circulates vital nutrients within the Earth and within our bodies. As long as the water is clean, then nourishment is wholesome. When it becomes fouled even the best of foods can become poison. Cleansing our emotions is necessary if we are to receive without distortion. Often what is given is contaminated by old tendencies still circulating in our system. Releasing to the inevitability of our return cleanses our resistance and flushes ancient toxins from the system.

Danger develops skills which often become our greatest strengths. Perseverance in the face of danger allows us to penetrate to the heart of a situation and assures success. Water flows no matter what the danger. Our will to understand must remain a steady river within if we are to negotiate the difficult terrain of the spiritual journey.

The vitality necessary to complete our journey is intimately connected with our emotional health. The danger in rectifying emotional trauma is that, often, the very act of investigation removes us from the greater flow of life and makes healing impossible. Repairing the torn places of our hearts requires a fine balancing act between remembering the pain and staying grounded in our present creative expression. If we succumb to the memory, we run the risk of drowning. If we avoid the memory, we run the risk of living incomplete lives. Anchoring to the eternal flow of Water, we can achieve this necessary balance.

Fluid and always true to ourselves, we return to our source…

Touching deeply,
eventually flames must ignite.
Coming close,
we penetrate the surface
and Fire is the result...

30

The Clinging (Fire)

Fire clings to its source,
consuming matter
to create light.
Illumination
comes with clarity,
and clarity comes
from truth.
Clinging to what is right
we have an inexhaustible source
of nourishment.

When our Fire within
burns brightly
then the Fire is seen
everywhere
and in all people.

Consuming
Penetration
Clarity

The Clinging (Fire)

Fire above: Perception, Clarity   Fire below: Perception, Clarity

The world is made visible by virtue of the Fire of the sun; the orbit of the Earth is fixed by the mass of the sun. This relationship illustrates the nature of clinging. We are illuminated by that which has great weight. In the eastern traditions, the word "guru" (or teacher) also means heavy. Some of the heaviest elements known are also the most fiery (e.g. uranium).

In order to liberate light, we must understand clinging. Fire clings to that which burns; lovers cling to one another and dissolve individuality; a student clings to the teacher and is transformed. Attraction is an inherent power in the universe. Gravitation is one of the prime conditioning forces of celestial mechanics and it is a product of the attraction between bodies of great mass.

The I Ching illustrates how this all-too-human failing is actually a profound secret of transformation. If we close the gap between ourselves and the world, then we merge the perceiver and the perceived. This union is a spiritual Fire of great magnitude. Only by burning away the cloak of appearances can we enter into the heart of reality. This penetrating perception is the gift of Fire. Clinging to the surface of wood, Fire begins to consume the very object which is its source.

In our relationships, if we burn away the projections of our old family patterns, then we can truly see one another for the light of which we are made. The Fire of a new relationship exists precisely because we have not yet erected the masks of memory and fear, and we are willing to dance in the center of the dance where the heat is intense. There is a burning that begins in any relationship which sears away distortion and projection. If we can stand the heat, then we can emerge as light from the process.

The luster of creation is formed by the Fire which burns in all beings and all forms. When this Fire dies, the world is boring, two dimensional, and without meaning. When this fire burns, then the world is endowed with beauty and depth.

To see the universe in a grain of sand takes an interior inferno. We must have such a Fire to burn away the gross and release the subtle. This spiritualization of our vision is the gift of Fire.

Penetrating to the core, Fire is released…

The Fire of the heart
brings together
the masculine and feminine.
The mystery of
their relationship
is the domain of Influence...

31

Influence (Wooing)

The Mountain's strength
gives form to the Lake.
The Waters of the Lake
nourish and give life
to the Mountain.

Mutual attraction between a man and a woman
arises as they perceive
the completion of themselves
in the mirror of their partner.
Constancy and perseverance
advance the relationship
beyond courtship
and make the
Influence
enduring.

Attraction
Stimulation
Courtship

Influence (Wooing)

Lake above: Joy   Mountain below: Stillness

The Waters of the Lake nourish the Mountain, and the Mountain gathers clouds to fill the Lake: this mutual support is called Influence. The strength of the Mountain supports the joy of the Lake. The Lake, symbolic of the youngest daughter, and the Mountain, symbolic of the youngest son, are in the process of Wooing one another.

Attraction that does not degenerate into seduction and co-dependency is based on an Influence which supports both the man and the woman. The humility of the masculine creates a chalice for the feminine, and the Waters of the feminine wash through the man with heavenly moisture. The top of the Mountain is a crater which forms the womb of the Lake. Strength has, as its ultimate expression, humility. This receptivity makes for an Influence which is far-reaching and supportive of the feminine. The woman, in return, waters the center of the man with her depth. This happens mysteriously and beyond conscious awareness. If the Influence is built upon mutual respect, then both are strengthened by the gift. If the Influence is self-serving, then the woman can drown the man's emotional response and dominate him to the point of harshness. If the man is not pure in his Influence, then he can attempt to enslave the woman, forming boundaries with his power that are severe and inappropriate to the situation.

By keeping still within and expressing joy without, we can attract situations which are a reflection of our strength. Having a firm foundation within, we can be receptive without. Trusting in our own essence, we can mingle with others, receiving nourishment without fear of attachment.

Attraction without attachment is the secret to proper Influence. Attraction is an essential force in the universe, acting at a molecular as well as human level. Attraction leads to new bonds and new structures. If we meet those situations with our strength firmly in place, then the result is favorable.

Crater Lake in Oregon is remarkable for the intensity of its blue waters. It is as if the sky itself had come down to the Earth and taken up residence. This is a powerful image of a man and woman forming a harmonious relationship on the wings of true Influence. Both lives are enriched by the essence of the other: purity, harmony, and greater beauty are the hallmarks of the union.

An innate humility allows our minds to remain free; we are then able to receive wise counsel. This is symbolized by those superior people who are willing to hear counsel and are not arrogant in their strength. Such a position is one which assures favorable Influence.

Through humbleness, lasting Influence is achieved…

113

Courtship leads to a lasting
connection of the heart.
This marriage,
both inwardly
and outwardly,
is manifested by Duration…

32

Duration

The planets circle endlessly in orbit,
the seasons flow
one into the other,
the Winds of the Heavens
move endlessly;
these are the images of Duration.

What endures in our lives
is often near the truth.
In order to touch
the eternal
we must be patient.

To be patient
we must
breathe with the Winds
and study the cycles of the Tao.

Annual
Continuous
Patience

Duration

Thunder above: Movement, The Arousing   Wind below: Gentleness, Penetration

Wind blows and Thunder rolls: the two support one another and are a complete cycle of movement. Without the Winds, clouds cannot gather; without the clouds, Thunder cannot form; and without Thunder, the Winds grow complacent and die away.

The gentleness of the Winds supports the arousing Thunder. If our beginnings are based on gentleness and are in harmony with the Tao, then what has come into being will be carried to completion. Duration is the stability of knowing that cycles will be fulfilled. Not fearing commitment, we are able to complete each cycle in our lives. This inner steadiness is a source of great strength.

So often we weaken ourselves by premature commitment and abort necessary growth out of fear of entrapment. The continuous motion of the Heavens is ever free, and yet is contained within the weather patterns. We need not fear the constraint of commitment because there is the possibility of great movement. Winds dance and lightning strikes: these are vital, forceful movements which enliven and inspire. Duration is the condition which allows real freedom.

Continuity instills a quality of faith. The cycles of the seasons, of the planets, and of our own breath are the fundamental rhythms which organize the world around us. This is a sacred perception: seeing the cycles of growth and change continuously revolving, we are able to rest in the arms of nature.

Devotion born of Duration is strong and unswayed by the fickleness of the mind or the impulsiveness of the emotions. Anchored in the immutable cycle of change, we have the courage to remain firmly on the path.

Duration is the quality whereby dedicated individuals form the world around them in response to the clarity of their inner knowing. This steady and continual application of inner truth to the world is the secret of any successful enterprise. Work then helps meaning to become manifest and is no longer a burden or an imposition on the creative spirit.

Duration is the power of eternal return…

The continuous cycle of life
circles through darkness and light,
rising and falling, advancing and retreating...

The continuity of life
is often best seen from a position of Retreat...

33

Retreat

Withdrawing from the exterior world,
we form the seeds of our new beginnings
quietly
and in the solitude of the Heavens.

Cultivating stillness,
we can retire from our daily routine
and touch more essential heights.

Withdrawing from the world
is not the same as escape.
Withdrawal leaves only
a whisper in its wake
and is the doorway
of the spirit.

Withdrawal
Seed Form
Interior

Retreat

Heaven above: Strength, Creativity   Mountain below: Stillness

There are times when the external world is no longer the appropriate field of action. The work which must be done is very subtle and very much inside. This subtlety is like the blue sky of a clear day. Looking towards the sky, we cannot distinguish the source of the color; it is a subtle emanation of light and atmosphere. Such delicate inner tasks are best done away from our worldly concerns and interactions.

There are times to learn from our involvements, and there are times when our involvements entrap us in projections and reactions based on endless unconscious motives. Retreat is the call of space, the stillness of the mountain top. Only in such a pristine world can the truly subtle be felt and formed.

Retreat is not escape. Retreat is a withdrawal of energy and a consolidation of purpose. Often in our cycle of growth, it is necessary to find our limits by spending time alone, without the reflection of others. This work is akin to climbing a difficult Mountain; it demands the utmost attention and focus.

In solitude we can gain the poise to truly understand our own inner mechanism. We have freedom from intrusion to be able to follow our own thoughts and feelings to their very end. There may be great voids and difficult walls of stone, but having scaled all of them, we will be welcomed by Heaven itself. We will have the strength to step away from the physical world and exist purely in the realm of subtle idea and energy.

A true Retreat is not a passive act, but a strenuous, active climb. If it becomes passive, then it runs the risk of becoming an escape. Escaping from our problems will only weaken us and turn into a collapse of force. Retreat is right only when we clearly see the field we are leaving behind. To turn and run blindly will only bind us to the very issues from which we are hoping to escape.

Withdrawing in stillness, we can touch the subtle truths of the Heavens. Gathering in the Winds of the Heavens are the seeds of future actions. Gathering the Heavens deep inside, we are made ready for the next cycle of our lives.

Withdrawing into the subtle, we gain the strength to transform our worlds…

119

Having touched the subtle,
we return to the world
with Thunder as the gateway.

Expressing what has been
gathered in solitude,
we enter The Power of the Great…

34

The Power of the Great

Thunder fills the Heavens:
this is The Power of the Great.
Acting in accord with the Tao,
strength brings illumination
and does not degenerate
into mere force.

Creative action
thunders across the Heavens.
This is a time of rising inner worth.
Mindful of possible arrogance
we execute our tasks
with precision and
power.

Exaltation
Ascendancy
Power

The Power of the Great

Thunder above: Movement, The Arousing   Heaven below: Creativity, Strength

Thunder rolls across the Heavens: this is the image of great power. This denotes a time in our lives when our personal power has gathered sufficient strength to demonstrate itself clearly and decisively. There can be no doubting the force of lightning as it strikes from the Heavens. From a strong accumulation of power we need not fear opposition and are in a position to effect great change.

It is at these cusp points that we must be most alert, for strength can degenerate into force if we are not aware of the proper course of action. This course is determined by the timing of events. Lightning is so swift that it must be released at precisely the right time or it will dilute its effect. A flash of awareness can be lost in the sky if it is not linked to timely action.

The Power of Greatness bears tremendous responsibility. An understanding of the inner order of events is necessary to ensure a fruitful outcome. Ultimately, all power flows from sources far beyond our personalities. The proper contemplation of the source of our power is essential if we are not to abuse it. Hitler was possessed by his power and lost all human response; Mother Teresa cultivated a profound humility in the face of the Divine, and, consequently, her power has nourished and healed others.

Power can grip our lives like lightning. We can be swept away by its current before we even realize the consequences. When power is on the rise we would do well to continually contemplate the source of our movement, and stay in touch with that which is greater than ourselves. There are thunderstorms in Arizona which are so severe that lightning is striking almost continuously. In the face of such power it is not difficult to remember our position in the universe. The Hopi, who live with lightning as their temple flames, have a profound reverence for the order of nature and their place in creation. And yet, their legends tell us that it is they who literally hold the world together. This world-making power can only flow through a receptacle which is in harmony with a more profound order.

Thunder resounds because it has the Heavens as its drum. The arousing Thunder striking The Creative sets all of creation into reverberation. The Power of the Great is none other than the original impulse of creation taking form.

The drum beat of creation has risen to the Heavens…

Riding the wave of ascending power,
we are carried high
and it is inevitable that we
will make Progress…

35

Progress

Fire rising steadily above the Earth
is the image of Progress.
The sun as it climbs
dispels darkness.
The light of understanding
floods the shadows
within our hearts.

We must align ourselves
with a rising principle
in order to ensure Progress.
What is clear in the Heavens
becomes right action
on Earth when
received with humility.

Steadiness
Alignment
Gradual Ascent

Progress

Fire above: Clarity, Perception   Earth below: Devotion, Receptivity

Fire rising over the Earth: the image of the sun as it steadily climbs into the Heavens. Leaving the affairs of the Earth behind, we are able to uncover the essential light within. The conditioning of earthly experience must be systematically purified so that our true radiance can shine.

The dawning of light begins as a whisper of color in a starlit sky. The steady and measured progress of the sun assures a blanket of warmth for the coming day. Birds awaken, sleep is put aside, and Progress is inevitable.

This is a time for releasing old patterns, retiring outmoded ways of moving in the world, and rising with the sun. When light is ascending, the shadows of old conditions fall away naturally. During times of Progress, self-analysis can be most productive. Since Progress is assured by the timing of events, difficult issues of inner turmoil can be tackled.

The day gathers light as it progresses: this is natural and a gift of celestial movement. Linking the action in our lives to an organic order will enable us to transform even the most difficult of situations.

It is the devotion of the Earth which supports the rising of the Fire. On the wings of faith, flames soar to the Heavens. Change that is rooted in a deeply receptive heart is in accord with the Tao. Cultivating the Earth, we are able to harvest much growth at the end of the season. Tending to the fields of our lives with devotion, we open the floodgates of Progress.

Fire shines on the surfaces of creation. The illumination of the external opens the way to perceiving inner light. This rising of the inner light is the benediction of Progress. Assured of outer illumination, we are inspired to pursue our spiritual work.

Progress in our relationships means remaining open to the blossoming of love. The seeds of future growth are sown early in any true meeting. There is a natural unfolding of relationship which assures the steady Progress of love within our hearts. Trusting in this process is the best protection against impulsive reaction. The warmth of the sun floods our hearts with hope and new promise.

The rising sun brings light to all lands upon the Earth…

Expanding with the rising light,
we can expect to encounter
resistance.
When this resistance
meets our Progress within
then we have Darkening of the Light...

36

Darkening of the Light

In times of outer darkness
we must return to the warmth of our hearts.
During such times external vulnerability
will lead to injury.

The Fire within the Earth
burns and yet does not lead
to great illumination.
The deep roots of our nature
burn hot and yet
it is not a time for visible expression.

Containment
Protection
Inside

Darkening of the Light

Earth above: Devotion, Receptivity   Fire below: Clarity, Perception

Fire has fallen into the Earth: the image of Darkening of the Light. A wounding has taken place and it is essential that one's light be protected. There are wounds that are healed by taking action and there are wounds that are healed by going on retreat. This is the condition of the latter.

Protected by a mantle of devotion, it is possible to rekindle the damaged Fire and heal old wounds. Giving thanks for the gifts of the Earth helps establish an organic ground that can repair very tender wounds (in the Native American tradition, prayers and chants invoke the four directions of the Earth in order to establish a sanctuary of healing). The deepest wounds cannot be healed by analysis. These are wounds which touch the core and cannot be resolved by the mind. They ask us to release old and inappropriate ways of living. This sacrifice is an act of devotion, not a mere act of reflection.

These wounds are often a limitation which is the soil of future greatness. The wounds which heal are the wounds of the sacred. Light is darkened, and this journey of the night is often a gateway to spiritual illumination and transcendence. Is it not often darkest just before the dawn?

The power of the Earth and the humility of a receptive heart are the qualities needed to heal us in this situation. If we follow the track of our wounds deep enough, then we can understand their connection to the sacred. This journey takes a heart that can feel and receive the whispering of the Tao itself. To hear this voice we must be quiet; we must be still and gather the protection of the Earth around us. The crucible of our healing is formed by the shielding of our light. It is not a proper time to venture out into the world. It is a time to plunge deep inside and protect our inner Fire. This folding inwards is a necessary prelude to any healing: the body contracts to heal injured parts; the psyche wraps whole behavior patterns around emotional wounds to help protect them.

Fire that is injured runs the risk of vanishing in the slightest Wind. If we are to read the message of the flickering flames, we must give them protection. Then, in the womb of the Earth, we can take the healer's journey and trace our wounds back to their sources. This undertaking is ultimately a spiritual matter. A return to the sacred is the only recourse we have when our Light is being Darkened.

Darkening of the Light means surrendering to the depth of our receptivity: feeling the wounds as well as the Fire that burns in our hearts. This is a warrior's compassion: a rich and multilayered quality of love that emulates the heartbeat of the Earth.

Returning to the arms of the Earth, we can heal…

In times of injury
a circle of trusted hearts
is often the best instrument of healing.

The closest circle,
our foundation hoop,
is our Family…

37

The Family

Just as the warmth of the sun creates the
Winds of the world,
so the inner warmth of a Family
can influence all who bask in its light.

The most penetrating influence
is achieved by developing inner heat;
the Family is the crucible
for this work.

Honoring the Fire which rises
between a man and a woman,
the Family flourishes.

Foundation
Crucible
Home

The Family

Wind above: Gentleness, Penetration   Fire below: Clarity, Perception

Fire burns with clarity and warmth. From this central heat, Wind is stirred and carries affection to the world. The heart of a Family is formed by the clinging Fire. The closeness of the Family members generates a heat which has many forms: affection, friction, inspiration, clarity, turbulence, and the gentle Fire of emotional well-being. Learning to dance with the different flames keeps the Family dynamic and yet bonded. From the inner Fire of the Family, the effect is carried on gentle Winds to others, and ultimately to society at large.

If the home Fire is erratic and burns hot and cold, then the disturbance is carried beyond the home and creates turbulence in many lives. Burning too hot, the boundaries of Family members are dissolved and passions flare up to obscure the underlying affection of the heart. Burning too cold, the distance between Family members becomes too great, and estrangement, isolation, and emotional starvation occur.

The gentle Wind is what blows from a harmonious Family. The compassion and affection of the Family is founded on the steady Fire of daily interaction. Within the cauldron of the Family, one learns of the balance between personal space and communal needs. This helps to instill a moral balance which creates inner freedom. Carrying the warmth of the Family into their separate lives, each member is nurtured from the central flame and flourishes in society.

The inner order of Fire follows exact laws of nature, and yet is fluid rather than rigid. Brilliance and clarity shine forth from an organic order. So, too, in our Families. Light will shine from a Family structure that intuitively follows the laws of nature. Every Fire needs room to breathe, and yet the logs must be close enough to keep the Fire burning. Finding the correct balance between personal needs and the overall function of the Family is essential.

The warmth of the heart is easily wounded by Family dysfunction. The injuries in a Family setting dim the light of all Family members. We have a duty to attend diligently and gracefully to the Family fire, for the warmth of the Family is one of the greatest healing forces in our lives.

The Fire of the home is the warmest of all…

An incomplete Family
leaves residue
which appears as inner tension.
This tension
when brought to our current
relationships
produces Opposition…

38

Opposition

Fire flames upwards
and a Lake's Waters flow downwards:
this is the image of Opposition.

When tendencies are clearly
moving in different directions
it is best to let the situation
mature of its own accord.

Allowing Opposition,
we can resolve conflict by
understanding the necessity for differences.

Releasing our need to control,
we can ride the wave of Opposition
to a peaceful conclusion.

Individual Movement
Differences
Destiny

Opposition

Fire above: Clarity, Perception   Lake below: Joy

Fire burns upwards and the Water of the Lake seeps downward: these are images of two movements which are in Opposition. When a situation is clearly opposed, it is best to let the tendencies resolve themselves through their differences.

All of nature is held in balance by Opposition: day and night, male and female, hot and cold, joy and sorrow, high and low. There are times when situations must be made clear through an understanding of the inherent differences rather than seeking a common ground of accord. In honoring Opposition it is important to remember the essential polarities of our existence. Only in the tension of opposites is the manifest world able to hold its form. A premature collapse of tension produces chaos and impedes healthy development.

Opposition clarifies boundaries and helps establish individual identity. Without the Fire of Opposition it is difficult to cultivate an honest sense of one's own being. Opposition requires that we come to know our own nature by seeking the true source of conflict. If tension is present and our own heart is tranquil, then we know that something beyond our own ken is at work. On the other hand, if our own flame is weak and fraught with internal inconsistency, then we must do the necessary inner work of understanding the Opposition within ourselves.

Opposition is often necessary in order to achieve union. We must remember this paradox and not weaken ourselves with despair. Only when we have been fired by Opposition and tempered by having plunged deeply into our watery nature will we be strong enough to meet another.

It is important during times of Opposition to allow the process to unfold. Removing ourselves because it feels uncomfortable or difficult will not resolve the Opposition. True Opposition is one of the cornerstones upon which the material world is built. We must not hesitate to encompass the world of opposites within our own being and have the strength to be made truly whole.

Remember that the flames dance above the Waters of the Lake as a symbol of potential reconciliation. Water remains Water and Fire remains Fire, yet they dance together in a dramatic display of light and shadow on the Lake. This is the inherent joy of Opposition. Cultivate this joy to gain strength.

Maintaining the tension of Opposites, we are made whole…

As the tension of
Opposites increases we are often
confronted with obstacles
designed to strengthen us
and lead us towards wholeness.

The will to persist despite
such blockage is the
lesson of Obstruction…

39

Obstruction

Dangerous Waters
before us
and Mountain cliffs behind us:
the image of Obstruction.

Turning within
to understand the inner source
of our obstacles,
we are reconnected
with the current of our will.
Obstructions ask us to reflect more completely
on the nature of our own movement.
The still, strong, quiet
of the Mountain is
our ally in this
journey.

Inner Resources
Internalization
Courage

Obstruction

Water above: Danger, The Abyss   Mountain below: Keeping Still

A Water's flow is blocked by a Mountain: the image of Obstruction. Obstructions arise in order to turn us back upon ourselves. The hindrances we experience in life ask us to consult our friends and seek wisdom in order to rectify the situation.

Obstruction is often the result of isolation. In believing that we are self-sufficient, when in fact we are actually afraid of seeking support, we create a serious illusion. This illusion is often shattered by an immovable obstacle which is placed in our pathway. The stillness of a Mountain cannot be manipulated or seduced into cooperating with our self-serving ambitions. In its stillness, the Mountain is free from guile and self-serving tendencies. This is a hint as to what needs to be cultivated in the face of an obvious obstacle.

Turbulent emotions, which obscure basic stillness, create the desire for fulfillment when, in fact, they are taking us further from that possibility. It is at this juncture that major obstacles appear to direct us back to our essential truth. Water cascading down a Mountain gains power and momentum, but can also be dangerous and uncontrollable. It meets obstacles along the way that tame its turbulence and invite a new measure of peace and repose. A Lake is born by virtue of the Obstruction of the Earth. A Lake rests in its own nature until it is full, then it spills over to continue the journey home.

We are asked to seek counsel when obstacles appear. Realizing that we have exhausted our own momentum, it is time to appear in humbleness at the Sage's door. So often it is the pain and blockage in our lives which finally shatter our illusion of knowing and gives us the humility to seek help from others. These obstacles are actually jewels along the way. Obscured by our own resistance, they appear to be menacing and detrimental to our growth. Once we have turned to a greater wisdom, their true nature appears and we can appreciate the clarity and perfection of their position in our lives.

A willingness to honor the obstacles in our lives as emanations of wisdom is the magic key to unlocking their purpose. The Buddhists visualize elaborate inner demons in precise detail in order to honor the obstacles on the path. This practice helps the seeker. A clear vision of our obstacles opens the doorway to a wisdom that cannot be arrived at through impulsive action.

Obstruction stands at the threshold of true humility…

137

When our Obstacles have
wrought their revolution
and our hearts are turned
toward their source,
the way is made
for Deliverance...

40

Deliverance

The strain of a long and difficult time
is released in a swift and decisive manner.
Thunder resounds as it breaks
the tension of the storm.

With this resolution our actions
become direct.
We are no longer mired
in the darkness of hidden motives
and undetected currents.

In this circumstance,
Resolution is a gift
of the Heavens.

Resolution
Completion
Decisiveness

Deliverance

Thunder above: Movement, The Arousing   Water below: Danger, The Abyss

Rainfall releases the tension of a thunderstorm: the image of Deliverance. When faced with danger we begin to move. By moving, we are delivered from a difficult situation.

This hexagram speaks to the fine balance between personal and Divine will. We cannot move from difficult situations in our lives if we do not take action; and yet, the greatest movement is often made by a gift of grace. A sudden release of accumulated tension is triggered by a strike of lightning and a downpour of rain. This emptying of the Heavens for the benefit of the Earth is symbolic of the descent of grace in our daily lives.

In order to prepare for this Deliverance, we must recognize the danger which is before us. Danger takes the form of unclear motives, imprecise agreements, and a murky sense of direction in our life's flow. This confusion is a result of muddy waters: stirred emotions that obscure clarity can suck us into deadly whirlpools of repetitious situations. Seeing clearly the danger before us, we are stirred into action and we mobilize our personal will to move us out of the abyss. It is at this moment that the Heavens open and the thunderstorm descends. The Earth is bathed in Water and the skies are clear. Deliverance is at hand.

Being asleep to the danger before us, giving in to inferior feelings and emotional turbulence, we do not prepare the way for Deliverance. We must already be moving or the motion of a thunderstorm may overwhelm us and feel like a flood instead of a nourishing rain. From the perspective of inertia, Deliverance often feels dangerous. All too often, people who are blind to the danger of their situation fall asleep and resent the lightning of the Heavens when it strikes. Without the proper preparation, Deliverance can fall on unprepared soil and be gone.

Flash floods occur when the Earth is hardened and cannot accept the burden of Water. Raging walls of Water then turn upon the landscape and race homewards, unable to slake the thirst of the very desert which longs for rain.

We must be willing to move if Deliverance is to be seen for what it truly is: a descent of Waters from Heaven. A hardening of attitude changes the dynamic, liberating quality of the Heavens into a dangerous storm. This is the real tragedy of resistance, when it becomes a way of life.

Open and receptive to the Heavens, we can embrace the Thunder and rain, and quicken our growth with their gifts…

When the tension is released
new stability is found.
Though often not dramatic,
these times
are the foundations of new growth.

The secrets of the Mountain
are brought low
to the plains
in times of Decrease...

41

Decrease

There are times of plenty
and there are times of scarcity.
We should learn to recognize
a time of Decrease and tame our passions
accordingly.

A whole Mountain
is contained in
the reflection of a Lake;
likewise many great ideas
and vast movements
can be realized in small
and simple actions.
Decrease allows us to distill
the essence of action
and move
with simplicity and ease.

Reduction
Self-sacrifice
Distillation

Decrease

Mountain above: Stillness   Lake below: Joy

The Waters of a Lake rise to become clouds upon the Mountain: a time of Decrease. Decreasing what is below for the benefit of what is above is an essential task in spiritual development. Joy unchecked can lead to a passionate embrace of desire. Endless desires drain one's life force and lead to exhaustion. The Waters of joy, when elevated to the Mountain peaks, produce a passionate stillness, pregnant with potential and possibility.

The stillness of the Mountain without the joy of the Lake can lead to anger. A continued stance of quietude in the face of the numerous shocks of life can breed deep resentment. This resentment must be balanced by joy, otherwise the Mountain will be overbearing.

The Lake contains an image of the Mountain within its Waters. This is the Decrease of what is above. The ability to distill the essence of something much greater and to contain that essence in an image accessible to our daily world is demonstrated here. The Lake reflects events in the Heavens and nourishes the Heavens with its Waters.

Proper distillation is a critical task. All too often in our lives, we abandon qualities which have not yet fully developed in an effort to reach the mountaintops. This aggressive Decrease of our nature may ultimately weaken our foundation and lead to a collapse. Moderation in directing our impulses and curbing our desires is as important as the work of Decrease itself.

Inspiration congealed into an image, word or idea is necessary in order to help guide our distilling process. If we have glimpses of the Heavens, we are more likely to curb impulsive action and set about for the work of inner development. The joy of the Lake helps personalize the abstract realms of the Heavens and inspires us to continue the journey.

In relationships, our ability to give assures a continued flow of support. Stilling anger and curbing impulsive emotional outbreaks build a subtle yet strong capacity for real communication. Excessive Decrease leads to repression, but proper containment helps develop true strength and commitment. Knowing when to give and when to remain still is important in establishing proper boundaries. Healthy boundaries assure longevity in relationships.

What is below is Decreased for the benefit of what is above, and what is above is Decreased for the inspiration of what is below. This is the dance of Heaven and Earth, and is fundamental to the changes in our lives…

Distillation produces potency,
potency increases will,
and great will brings Increase...

42

Increase

Increasing what is light
and releasing what is dark
we gradually transform
our character.

When the highest
serves the lowest
all of creation
is blessed.

Thunder and Wind
Increase one another
and saturate the Heavens.

Discernment
Advancement
Service

Increase

Wind above: The Gentle, Penetrating   Thunder below: Movement, The Arousing

Wind precedes Thunder, and Thunder spawns the Winds: this is the image of Increase. An additional quality of Increase is suggested by the one solid (yang) line that has entered the hexagram from below. The Creative, by virtue of giving up its lowest line, becomes the gentle Wind. The Receptive, in accepting one yang line from Heaven, becomes Thunder. The decrease of Heaven produces gentleness, the Increase of Earth creates Thunder.

Increase is the inevitable result of service. When what is above serves what is below, all benefit from the exchange. In serving one another, we are able to open gently to the movement of the Tao. This gentleness is born of a humility which tempers The Creative and gives it energetic expression on the Earth.

True Increase never depletes its source. This is important to remember when assessing our level of service. If, in the name of giving, we find ourselves exhausted, burnt out, and unable to met our own needs, then we are not truly serving. In serving with the gentleness of a compassionate heart, Heaven flows through us and awakens the Earth we walk upon. We are uplifted by the service we perform, and this helps to establish the all-important link between The Receptive and The Creative.

When we are not gentle with ourselves, our service takes on an edge which cuts the hand that serves. The source of service is the gentle penetration of truth. Increasing our world through giving, we make Heaven on Earth. The Heavens give of themselves to the Earth through the gentle Winds of love. Thunder awakens our hearts to the gentleness which sustains them. We can serve because we are replenished in the act.

When the Heavens serve the Earth, then all are Increased. When we become instruments of this service, we are then given Nourishment which far exceeds what can be found when motivation is based on personal desire. We are moved like Thunder and penetrate like the Wind. As Gandhi demonstrated, even the strongest nations cannot stave off the Winds of true service. His was a Thunder that gave India her freedom.

Is this not Increase?

The Thunder of Increase reverberates with change…

Gathering power,
an Increase of light
leads to an abundance
in the Heavens.

When strength
is strengthened
a Breakthrough is inevitable...

43

Breakthrough

Moisture gathers in the Heavens,
thunderheads churn,
climbing thousands of feet
before the
Breakthrough.

After a long period of internal gathering,
the time has come to act.
When the Waters of our passions
are released through clear action,
great works are possible.

A Lake bursts from the Sky;
change is torrential.

Overburden
Release
Downpour

Breakthrough

Lake above: Joy   Heaven below: Strength, Creativity

A Lake bursts from the sky releasing built-up tension in a torrential downpour. The thunderclouds which build in the late afternoons of summer gather the heat of the day into monumental shapes which dominate the sky. This preponderance of activity eventually must be released. The rain which is born from such action can be overwhelming in its effect upon the Earth, thus the caution to be diligent in examining oneself during times of Breakthrough. Resolute action is necessary if tension is to be resolved in a way which is beneficial both on Earth and in Heaven.

When dealing with a situation that is a distortion of the truth, we must resolve to act with self-knowledge or a violent collapse may follow. Engaging the enemy without seeking their reflection in our own lives leads to endless aggression. Breakthrough signifies an end to a long period of turmoil and struggle. The tension of difficult times strengthens the creative impulse through resistance. It is only in transforming resistance that we are able to build fundamental strength in our lives. Resistance must be internalized and liberated within our own hearts, or else it will remain as a weight of anger upon us.

We form boundaries by resisting. Some are necessary and important in our growth, others are debilitating and imprison us in old beliefs and reactions. A child's resistance is dramatic and difficult, but quite necessary for his or her development. A government's resistance to change breeds rebellion and may lead to its eventual downfall. Knowing when to resist and when to receive is critical in forming healthy boundaries.

Breakthrough is a time when our resistance has culminated in action. If we have matured through the period of waiting, then our actions have strength and clarity. If we indulge in obstinate resistance, then our Breakthrough will be clumsy and potentially dangerous to others around us.

The floods of ancient Egypt laid a carpet of new soil which nourished the people for thousands of years. The annual renewal and devastation appeared in their art, tombs, religion, and racial character. Their attunement to the cycles of change led to dynasties which lasted hundreds of years. Seasonal Breakthroughs replenished their spirit and annually resolved long-standing conflicts.

A cloudburst washes the Earth clean and strips away old tendencies. Flash floods break out of stream beds and chart new courses. There is power and danger in such a time.

When the Heavens let go, the Earth is washed clean with new life…

New pathways are the gift
of Breakthrough.
When we are able to receive
in new ways we are Coming to Meet...

44

Coming to Meet

Our foundations are shaken
by a newly emerging
feminine force.
New ways to receive,
new responses,
new options
all rise to meet the light
of a new dawn.

In such times it is best
to be straightforward
and honest,
paring away cowardice
and fear.

World Shift
Emerging Feminine
Influx

Coming to Meet

Heaven above: Strength, Creativity   Wind below: Gentleness, Penetration

Gentleness comes from below and meets the strength of Heaven. This is a delicate time of transition. Strength must yield without becoming diluted, and gentleness must remain consistent or it will be overwhelmed. The Winds are able to stir the Heavens because they are the harbingers of change. Weather systems are a delicate balance of high and low pressure gradients; the difference between the two is their driving mechanism. When a single yin line enters five yang lines, there is a sudden change of weather and this gradient can be dangerous. Strong Winds can create unrest as well as bring new rains.

Between a man and a woman the emergence of the feminine is a delicate balance. The masculine can recoil and feel threatened by the sudden shift of its foundations. The feminine can feel overwhelmed and alienated by the preponderance of The Creative. If the meeting is not gentle and respectful, a woman may contract and withdraw, and a man may attempt to challenge and control.

The impulse of the feminine often follows deep patterns of intuition which may feel alien to the logical order of the masculine. A situation which has stabilized around the masculine tends to form predictable patterns. At their best, these patterns are elegant and streamlined containers for creative energy; at their worst, they are reactive and conservative bastions of domination and control. When the intuitive begins to shake the foundation, it can often feel frightening and dangerous to the masculine. It is best, then, that the feminine approach in gentleness, and that she trust her inherent ability to transform the situation. If she should grow fearful she may withdraw prematurely, which will only further alienate the masculine.

This is a time of temptation. Because of the radical shift of foundation, there is often an urge to manipulate and seduce in order to maintain control in a rapidly changing environment. A dark element is rising, and it is important not to give in to negative tendencies and habits. Such weakness of self-discipline will only increase the tension of an already difficult transition.

It is a courageous act when the feminine Comes to Meet the masculine. The Heavens themselves can be moved, and this is no small undertaking. Gently allowing the contact to mature into a full relationship is the best course of action.

Foundations are shaken by new receptivity…

When new meeting occurs
the seeds of community begin.
The currents of formation
are strong and bring Gathering…

45

Gathering

We gather together
when we see in those around us
the reflection of
the work we have done inside ourselves.
Such Gatherings become a testing ground
for our inner work,
a crucible of our transformation.

Individuals join together,
guided by mutual inspiration
and purpose.
A common heart
unites and creates
the possibility of community.

**One Heart
Mutual Accord
Destined Meetings**

Gathering

Lake above: Joy   Earth below: Devotion, Receptivity

The Waters of the Earth gather together to form Lakes. Similarly, people gather together to form communities and to execute like-minded tasks. Devotion to the expression of our communal purpose instills joy. The boundaries of Gatherings should be determined by the needs of the common purpose. Duty that springs from a mutual recognition and appreciation has a joyous quality that keeps the community fluid and ever-receptive to the Winds of the spirit.

Lakes gather in the wombs of the Earth. By recognizing our common purpose, we can nurture and protect our creative urges until they have the strength to stand on their own. This is one of the functions of community: to protect the members and help bring new ideas and forms into the world. Without the protection of a larger community, the individual can be left struggling for survival. Appreciation for our communities is a quality of devotion that will help heal our world and ourselves. All too often, we become estranged from the collective and run the risk of isolation and spiritual desolation.

Communion with the Tao is essential in molding and forming our communities. Worship should be a heartfelt and joyous Gathering of individuals. In celebrating our common respect for the spirit within each of us, we establish a bond of the heart that enriches our lives.

There is a tradition among the Eskimo peoples of adopting members of menacing villages as relatives. This extended web of relations, not all linked through blood-lines, allowed the Eskimos on the Bering Sea to live in peace for five hundred years. An invitation from the heart, for all to be our relations, is an acknowledgment of our common source. It will allow us to put down our weapons and join in mutual peace.

There is often a destiny to our Gatherings. Recognizing that we may have a purpose together which is greater than at first evident, is an important step in securing the foundations of our communities. Brought together by our mutual expression, we are able to live in peace with one another. Joyful in the devotion to our tasks, we can build a world that reflects the wisdom of the Tao.

Destiny runs deep when people Gather...

Established in the service
of our communities
we are able
to plant the seeds
of true spiritual aspiration.

Tending this growth
is the gift of Ascending...

46

Ascending

A tree's growth
is patient,
natural and enduring.
We should cultivate
such qualities
when applying ourselves
to spiritual transformation.

Pushing too hard
will damage one's growth;
resting too long
will arrest our development.
The right use
of will
is the foundation
of true Ascension.

Rising
Will
Spiritual

Ascending

Earth above: Devotion, Receptivity   Wind below: Gentleness, Penetration

A tree grows straight from the Earth guided by the knowledge of its own form. The desire to fulfill our potential is a motive which tempers our will and energizes our Ascension.

The journey from seed to treetop draws upon the strength of the Earth and the magnetism of Heaven. Growing towards light, we are pushed along our path despite obstacles and hindrances. Knowing when to push and when to be carried is the wisdom of true Ascent. A danger in being too receptive is that we are unable to move into action. Inertia is the legacy of devotion if one's will is weak. Forming deep intention, which is linked to our spiritual aspiration, is a balance for unchecked receptivity.

Fulfilling the promise inherent in each form is the voice of creation singing praise to its creator. Remembering the gift of our own form, our own seed, we can harness the vitality of growth itself to help us Ascend. The blueprint of our being is available for inspection through meditation and contemplation; in glimpsing the hidden maps of our own psyche we are anchored to the web of life. This web can be drawn upon for an inexhaustible supply of energy. This is one of the secrets of highly creative people.

Our temple of Ascension is our body. Reverence for the substance of our journey will temper the austerities and excesses of our travels. In body, we break through the soil and grasp the Winds with our branches, strong enough to give visible evidence of Creation's song. The central axis of our bodies pushes upwards to reconnect with the Heavens. The task of evolution rises to become conscious motive when we are linked to our spiritual aspirations. The grace of this movement carries us high above the Earth. We remain rooted and yet have access to the subtle currents of Heaven.

This growth is found in the right relationship between personal will and support from the outer environment. Initially this is our struggle as infants: the delicate task of balancing symbiosis with self-actualization. Referring back to the womb, we linger, afraid of the Ascent; plunging into self-determination, we often end up raging against the limitations of our world. As we mature, the Ascent becomes directed towards more abstract and subtle realms. It is at this junction that we are enjoined by the Book of Changes to seek wise counsel. Ascension is the principle of emergence that allows us to temper our wills with the patience of daily practice and steady progress. In seeing this principle displayed in nature we are inspired to continue our work of Ascent.

Gazing steadily upwards, we join the trees in their worship…

Our Ascent can be trying
and our journey long.
Tiring of this journey
there are times
when we experience Exhaustion...

47

Exhaustion

When a Lake can no longer
contain its Waters
Exhaustion has arrived.
It is best to now let fate
unfold
and not tire ourselves further
by needless resistance.
Following the Water's course
we will be taken
to a deeper place within
and new foundations
will be discovered.

Strain
Drain
Depletion

Exhaustion

Lake above: Joy   **Water below: Danger, The Abyss**

Water drains out of a Lake, leaving it dry and barren: this is the image of Exhaustion. Only in extraordinary times do Lakes dry up. Earthquakes and droughts give evidence of the severity of the times. There are moments in our lives when such extremes arise. These events can leave us exhausted.

When such events shake our world, it is important to cultivate joy in the face of the danger. Joy, in this context, is found by stripping away the non-essential and laying bare the fundamental ground of our lives. This is the fearless joy of one who no longer has anything to hide. The quality of the times has stripped away pretense and duplicity. The tension and struggle of maintaining facades is released as the Lake runs dry. Emotional undercurrents, which have obscured the truth, finally drain away and the bare bones of the Earth are left. One would think that a time of Exhaustion would lead to devastation and despair, but it need not; when all has been stripped away, new resolve and joy are possible.

When it becomes apparent that our lives are restructuring, we need to cultivate joy even though that may be difficult during the process of upheaval. Remembering that the process of draining away is the process of making ready for the new allows us to undergo the rigors of Exhaustion. Lakes seldom remain empty for long. They are containers which must assuredly be filled again. We should remember that the rains will come once more.

It is important to acknowledge our Exhaustion. If we fight the inevitable, then Exhaustion can lead to disease. To struggle when it is time to rest is to invite a more serious decline, one which may threaten the very fabric of our lives. Honoring our need to rest is a way of meeting the danger of such a decline. We will not truly rest unless we have cultivated trust in the cycles of the Tao. All life moves in cycles of fullness and decline. If we have studied the ways of Heaven and Earth, then we can place Exhaustion in its proper perspective.

What oppresses us is often what liberates us. This dialectic was known to successful revolutionaries throughout history. If we can travel to the depths of Exhaustion, then we have already begun our renewal.

In times of Exhaustion, we can discover our true foundations…

Taken to the depths,
we drink of the Waters
which have lain
waiting.

Drinking deeply
of The Well
we are able to continue
our journey...

48

The Well

Roots reaching deep into the Earth
draw Water upwards.
Our foundations are deep
and give great nourishment.
The deepest Wells
often bring forth
the purest Water.
We should not hesitate
in reaching to our core
in order to
draw strength
for our journey.

Foundations
Nourishment
Depth

The Well

Water above: Danger, The Abyss   Wind (Wood) below: Gentleness, Penetration

In ancient China, the villages were organized around a Well; although the buildings may have crumbled and fallen, the Well always remained as the heart of the community. Stability in nourishment comes when we draw from deep levels of being. The external world is ever-changing and to seek nourishment in externals is to invite disappointment. In drinking deeply of the Waters within, we are assured of a stable source of nourishment.

The Wood which carries the Water from the Earth must be whole in order to fully utilize the Well. Our gentleness and compassion must embrace our efforts to draw forth our inner Waters. Wood without heart is dry and dangerous. It takes us to the edge of the Well and urges us forward without giving us the proper container to continue the journey. Without a bucket the Well is useless. The container we fashion, through our studies and effort, must acknowledge the true source of inspiration. All too often scholarship inflates the containers, and then the true Water of life is made unavailable.

The wisdom of the ages is always waiting to be tapped, a steady and dependable source of nourishment within each one of us. If we draw forth this understanding, then not only do we benefit, so does the world around us. Ancient wisdom is simple and elegant and does not need embellishment to provide nourishment. The simple act of Wood dipping below Water is enough to bring this precious wisdom to the surface.

Modern technology has increased our access to knowledge beyond anyone's mental capacity to assimilate information. Implicit in this hexagram is a hint as to how to restore balance in the age of information overload. The simple act of drawing Water in a bucket from the Well can restore our inner knowing. This simplicity eases our thirst and brings a much-needed balance to the tyranny of a mind filled with too many ideas. A fundamental return to ancient wisdom and timeless knowledge will nourish weary minds in the modern world.

Wind below Water means a stirring of the depths. The gentle application of our hearts to the task of drawing forth emotional nourishment is needed if we are to succeed. Between friends, the Well is symbolic of the depth of feeling which is the eternal bond of friendship. This bond lasts no matter what the changing surface conditions and is a source of continual nourishment. Fighting to drink from the Well only damages the container and leaves everyone thirsty. It is important to remember that our source of nourishment is ultimately ageless and deep; we need to allow ourselves the time and space to draw gently from this legacy.

True nourishment runs deep…

164

Deep Wells of nourishment
must be cleansed
in order to bring renewal.

This cleansing
is often life-changing
and may have the qualities of a Revolution...

49

Revolution

Fire rises within the Lake:
Revolution.
When differences are
so complete as to stir
the deepest Waters of our being,
Revolution is at hand.
Becoming agents of change
we are charged with a grave
responsibility;
acting too quickly can damage;
acting too slowly
can foster decay.
Returning to the realm of its making
Fire rises to join the sun,
and Revolution is
the sign of its passing.

Transformation
World Change
Renewal

Revolution

Lake above: Joy   Fire below: Clarity, Perception

Fire in the Lake and Revolution is at hand. The clarity of Fire penetrates the depths of the Lake and stirs long-forgotten memories. This is a Revolution of insight. A clear and radiant view into the submerged and hidden forces of our lives brings about a Revolution of character.

Nothing can remain the same when Fire and Water meet. Old ways must be shed like a snake sheds its skin. Old habits and patterns may have been appropriate to the situation and may have been harmonious in their own season, but they serve no more. Fire consumes that which it touches, and the Lake itself is seething with change. These are times of complete and utter transformation.

Such abrupt change should only be attempted when the time is right. Premature Revolution leads to protracted aggression and has little chance of resolution. Waiting too long for Revolution polarizes all parties involved and is just as dangerous. The changing of the seasons brings a Revolution of light. The long winter months give way to the warmth of spring and the heat of summer. There is a Revolution in the Heavens and complete trans-formation on the Earth. From this perspective, change is necessary in order to assure the unfolding of cosmic order. Revolutions are an aspect of the dance of light and darkness. If we can welcome them, keeping in mind the need for new order and new ways, then we can integrate the changes with less anxiety and fear.

Fire meeting Water is the driving mechanism for weather systems. As the sun heats the oceans, rain clouds form which then nourish the Earth. Occasionally storms rage which bring devastation; this is nature's response to an imbalance on the Earth.

Our inner heat, the Fire of our love, raises the Waters of unconscious motive and hidden force. Purified, these Waters fall upon new Earth and bring new growth. This can feel, at times, like a Revolution. These Revolutions are necessary in the seasons of our relationships. Embracing change, we can withstand the rigors of Revolution.

Rapid change challenges the predictable world of our expectations…

When the Fires of Revolution
are flaming,
new crucibles are forged.
In these Cauldrons
the most fundamental
transformations are possible...

50

The Cauldron

In the Fire of change
we sacrifice our
pettiness and limitations.
This work needs
a container in order
to bear fruit.
If we accept the current
of our destiny,
then we will not hesitate
in moving forward
in our work.
This Cauldron is not
different from ourselves,
it is in fact our very
essence.

Alchemy
Structure
Sacred Form

The Cauldron

Fire above: Perception, Clarity   Wind below: Gentleness, Penetration

A sacrificial vessel is necessary in order to refine our personality. This vessel is the context of our lives: our work, our relationships, our physical bodies, our interactions. Honoring our crucible means honoring situations which life presents to us. Cultivating the strength to embrace the circumstances of our lives, even in the face of adversity, enables us to perform the ultimate sacrifice: ego-centered actions and needs are sacrificed to the divine Wind of inspiration and guidance.

Just as Fire is conditioned by the wood upon which it burns, so fate in our life is an emanation of our basic nature. Contemplating our deepest impulses will lead us to the eternal. If we strip away pretense and masquerade, then we can indeed begin to cleanse the Cauldron and make it fit for a sacred Fire. The Fire of our personal actions needs a steady fuel to be sustained; if we lose the thread of our destiny, then we are cast adrift on a sea of uncertainty and life becomes meaningless. Often our destiny will lead us in directions our conscious selves resist. This, then, becomes the great sacrifice: the giving of ourselves to the movement of life.

By honoring the circumstances of our lives, we honor the Cauldron which has been given. Oftentimes, in the name of change, we are ready to uproot the old and condemn the very blood which has given us birth. We honor our ancestors by acknowledging the sacred vessel of creation that has been passed down through the generations.

Repairing the Cauldron means correcting the defects and making whole that which has been damaged. This is an elegant image of true psychological work. We seek to make whole our vessel so that our sacrifice can be true and can take us to the Heavens. With an imperfect crucible, the Fires of transformation cannot burn hot enough to achieve the true alchemy of changing lead into gold. Such a transformation is achieved only after a proper firing: the proper congealing of tendencies and qualities into a tempered spirit and radiant body.

Taking the Cauldron to the temple means placing the work we have done on ourselves into the Fire of divine contact. This is best done in a temple. The temple is symbolic of the most sacred, the most holy: those places in our lives which are the purest, both inwardly and outwardly. With such purity, we will achieve a sacrifice worthy of a well-crafted crucible.

The crucible of change is the gift of our destiny…

170

When the sacred vessels are formed
and the Fires have congealed,
there comes a time
when that power must move.

This movement comes as Thunder...

51

The Arousing (Thunder)

Light descends
and Thunder rolls;
the image of the arousing.
Shocked
by the brilliance of The Creator,
we are made strong.
Trembling before the fullness
of creation
we have no
fears of difficulties and hardships.
Thunder awakens
a reverence for life
and we order our worlds accordingly.

Movement
Descent
Shock

The Arousing (Thunder)

Thunder above: The Arousing, Movement   **Thunder below:** The Arousing, Movement

Thunder and lightning are striking manifestations of the power of creation. Arising from their cloud temples, they descend in stunning brilliance to awaken the Earth below. This shock of awakening is in resonance with the primal awakening at the beginning of time.

We often encounter fear when the power of creation appears so near to our hearts. This fear is the threshold of respect. We need not let this fear immobilize us. Rather, we should follow the path of light laid down by the shocking immediacy of the times. In this instance, fear is the great teacher. We are humbled and, in finding humility, are able to trace the thread of creation as it weaves its way through all the forms of our lives. Cultivating a profound respect for the power of the Tao, we are able to temper our own excesses, and participate fully in the impulse of light as it gives form to accumulated power.

Awakened by the descent of lightning, we have the eyes to see the luminosity of the world around us. We often let the daily fears and worries of our lives cloud our vision, and we lose the ability to see life as the vital gift that it is. When the power of the arousing is present, then we can no longer sleep. The dullness of our daily routine is splintered by the inescapable power of creation stirring.

Often lightning appears in our lives in the guise of disaster and misfortune. Sudden accidents and injuries are the tracks of lightning as it streaks across our inner landscape. When we are brought near to death, we are actually given life. It is not easy to stand next to a lightning strike, but it is a tempering which will bring new movement and new inspiration to our lives.

Where there is movement, there is life. Where there is extreme movement there is often an awakening. When such urgency arrives we move with the impulse and trust the eventual outcome. If we brace against the descent of this power, then we run the risk of annihilation. We cannot stand in the path of light and remain unchanged.

Lightning strikes and flames of creation are kindled in our hearts…

173

After movement,
then comes rest,
and in the stillness
we rise steadily
to touch the Heavens
like a Mountain…

52

Keeping Still (The Mountain)

Maintaining inner stillness
we are able to perceive the subtle.
Movement has come, returned
to its source.
The feminine descends
and the masculine rises,
each returning
to its source.
When motion stops,
then the inner workings of
the world
become visible
and meditation has matured.

Stillness
Retiring
Contemplation

175

Keeping Still (The Mountain)

Mountain above: Stillness   Mountain below: Stillness

The Mountain remains stable for eons. Seasons change, empires rise and fall, snows fall and snows melt, and yet the Mountain remains still. Stillness of the heart takes enormous strength. Desires and impulses rise and fall in the chamber of the heart. Keeping Still, we do not act upon the urges which arise. Such strength needs a firm foundation or it can become too harsh. Struggling to control impulses which arise out of insecure foundations often leads to debilitating criticism. The Mountain rests on the foundations of the Earth itself. Such support allows inner stillness to arise as a reflection of wholeness and not as an imposition of frustration and tyranny.

Keeping Still speaks of a posture which assures fundamental contact with life. The quiet of the body becomes the quiet of the mind, and in such silence the essential truths become evident. This is the posture of meditation.

When the currents leading to the outer world begin to coalesce around inner experience, then a stillness is born which takes us to the threshold of the self. With this posture, stillness is possible in action as well as quietude. Moving when it is time to move, and resting when it is time to rest, assures us of tranquility in all arenas of life.

Keeping Still, between friends, means ending constant reactivity and basing contact on respect and love. From inner stillness our hearts can rest in each other's presence. The foundation of our relationship is rooted in the Earth, and our communication is subtle, like the light at high altitudes. Above timberline, time begins to slow down and light dances freely amongst the stillness of the peaks. The noise of the everyday world is left below, and the mind comes to rest on the essential beauty of creation.

At the end of each breath is a moment of silence, which opens to the eternal. This inner sanctuary is prior to thought and prior to action. From this stillness each new wave of breath is born, each new impulse is brought forth. When our actions arise spontaneously from this stillness, then we have truly embodied the Mountain.

Cultivating stillness, we touch the Heavens…

Out of stillness
the seeds of growth arise,
steady and strong.

This movement is known as
Gradual Development…

176

53

Gradual Development

A tree grows slowly on a mountainside,
steadily gaining in strength
and enduring
season after season of change.
Gradual Development
builds a temple
of inner tranquility
by virtue of its measured pace
and by the eternity of its becoming.

Steady
Patient
Gradual

Gradual Development

Wind (Wood) above: Gentleness, Penetration   Mountain below: Stillness

A tree which grows at a high altitude is subject to an environment of extremes. As the seasons cycle through their changes, the tree is tested to the limits of its strength. This constant testing produces great strength and durability. Bristlecone pine trees live to be several thousand years old. These ancient sentinels are found high in the Mountains and are among the oldest living organisms on the planet. Their slow and Gradual Development parallels the unfolding of history since the time of Christ. The countless tests and storms of the last several thousand years have tempered the human soul, and are the legacy upon which we draw as planetary citizens.

When development proceeds slowly, then Heaven and Earth are fused together in the resulting form. This intermingling of realms is one of the primary tasks of our spiritual journey. Joining the vastness of the Heavens with the mantle of the Earth is a Promethean task, and one which can have dangerous results if hurried. The subtle transformation of our bodies is the result of the Fire of our spiritual practice. The spirit of the Bristlecone stands as a silent witness to the timelessness of this process.

Preparation for marriage should also be a time of Gradual Development. The joining of the masculine and feminine within our own hearts is one of the primary tasks of psychological and spiritual growth. The way to the wedding is found through a patient cultivation of both sides of our nature. When the two aspects of our being are full in their own expression, then the moment of union is possible. Cultivating the space of the feminine and the formation of the masculine is best done by remembering the legacy of the Bristlecone: slow and steady growth over long periods of time. This slow nurturing of our nature is essential, for we are, in fact, seeking to join the two primary forces of life.

True maturity is found when the eternal enters into the stream of time and slowly unfolds. Roots deep in the Mountain, branches touching the Heavens, and at the center of it all, an ancient tree of wisdom: this is the image of Gradual Development.

Wisdom gathered slowly weathers the strongest of storms...

Steadily gaining in strength
it becomes possible to
enter into marriage.
Knowing oneself,
patiently unfolding,
it is possible to then meet another:
The Marrying Maiden…

54

The Marrying Maiden

Affection is the energy of attraction
which underlies
all relationships.
Distilling this movement,
it then becomes possible
to join another.
The joy of the Lake and the power of Thunder
join together
in a celebration of union.

Vulnerability
Joy
Attraction

The Marrying Maiden

Thunder above: Movement, The Arousing   Lake below: Joy

Thunder in a Lake is a spectacle of light. Each ripple of Water reflects lightning as it flashes, shards of Fire upon the Water. Marriage marks the end of being a maiden. The entry into womanhood is announced by lightning piercing the Lake. This stirring of the Lake by heavenly forces is symbolic of an inner marriage which is taking place. The joyful and carefree attitude of youth is awakened by a heavenly force. This contact can be tumultuous, but it marks the beginning of a new maturity.

St. Theresa, St. John of the Cross, Ramakrishna, Rumi, and Kabir, all saints in their respective traditions, speak of contact with the Divine as a marriage with deeply sexual imagery. The awakening of the inner marriage (the offering of the inner feminine with devotion and the arousing masculine response) is symbolic of a spiritual awakening as well as a meeting of husband and wife.

The maiden is young and does not have the strength of experience to guide such a marriage. This is a perilous time for her, and yet, in the end, the rewards are great. Thunder cannot be contained nor controlled; it can only be experienced. This is a hint as to how to prepare for marriage. Cultivating inner receptivity builds the strength to withstand contact, which is born of the Fire of the Heavens. The Lake has depth enough to maintain its own nature and to reflect the Thunder of Heaven.

The Lake is associated with spring and Thunder is associated with autumn. What is born in the spring often dies in the autumn: a necessary death in order for new life to emerge. The two equinoxes, a time when light and dark are in balance, appear in the spring and fall. The maiden of spring marries a prince of autumn, and thus the year is arranged. Seasons change, lives meet, and yet the dance of yin and yang is constant. Remembering this, a maiden should meet in marriage with Joy and Enthusiasm. Something will die and something will be born; only the passage of time will make the journey clear.

Embracing thunder, joy is heard within and without…

Being available to relationship
we are available to life,
in being available to life
we are open to Abundance…

55

Abundance

Movement is supported by clarity
in a time of Abundance.
Seeing clearly what needs to be done
and then acting decisively
brings inner
and outer prosperity.
Fullness is a product
of ascending energy
and such ascent
is not eternal,
hence the need to appreciate
and honor
what is given
during this period.

Fullness
Ascendant
Complete

Abundance

Thunder above: Movement, The Arousing   Fire below: Clarity, Perception

Movement supported by clarity produces Abundance. Clearly seeing the course of our lives, we are able to attend to our work with energetic action. This clarity is born of deep introspection, and is the result of having burnt away fear, conditioning, and self-serving tendencies. When clarity is restored, then our internal Fire is bright, and its light guides our actions and the actions of others.

Abundance is a consequence of inner union, not of outer effect. The gathering of material goods should be in support of our service to life and not a bulwark against it. Linking clarity to action, we are able to move easily from intuition and inner knowing to outer functioning. This union is the true condition; Abundance is merely the effect.

There is an inherent danger in Abundance. The sun, having reached its pinnacle in the sky, must begin its descent. The moon, having become full, must begin to wane. When Abundance has crested, then we must be wary of its decline. The danger of materialism is that it entrances us with the reflection of light and we do not see the light itself. Cultivating the steadfast clarity of seeing light within all people and all objects, we can guard against the inner effects of such a decline. Often the second and third generations of wealthy families experience a loss of meaning and a lack of purpose which is translated into addiction and despair. This decline is an attribute of Abundance which need not take place if inner clarity is maintained through discipline and rigorous self-examination.

Abundance between friends means that we see each other clearly enough to act with tenderness, playfulness, and compassion. We can relax in the Abundance of love and the richness of our lives. From such relaxation, both energetic creative expression and spiritual wealth can flow. We must not become complacent during such times or we run the risk of falling asleep and letting the time of Abundance slip away.

Living fully in the Abundance of the world means being alive to colors, music, and form. The world is continually feeding our senses with a wealth of nourishment and stimulation. This nourishment can allow us to become a part of life, and no longer resist the movement of the Tao.

Embracing the cycles of our lives, we are vibrant with the fullness of life…

If fullness is found only
in external objects,
an inner restlessness
can often set
us Wandering…

56

The Wanderer

The Mountain remains
and the Fire wanders:
this is the image
of The Wanderer.
Fire without a home
burns brightly
yet does not always
produce warmth.
Wandering is helpful
in producing momentary illumination,
but not sufficient
for real change.

Eternal Youth
Homelessness
Journeys

The Wanderer

Fire above: Clarity, Perception   Mountain below: Stillness

Fire has no place to rest: the image of The Wanderer. Fire moves upwards and the Mountain resides in stillness; this is the condition of a Wanderer. When our perceptions cannot penetrate the stillness of our core, then we are driven by restless thoughts to wander upon the land in search of wisdom and guidance. Paradoxically, there is an education in wandering which often bypasses the hierarchy of traditional cultural structures. The motive for this education is a search for inner stillness. In youth, when perception has not yet been cultivated, it is difficult to penetrate to the core of events. The surface of reality is endlessly entrancing and leads one on a journey which has, as its ultimate destination, the stillness of one's own core. The myriad reflections of the outer world eventually lose their luster, and one is left with the silence of one's own soul.

A return to the Mountains is symbolic of this search for stillness. In the traditional Native American cultures, a youth would embark on a vision quest in order to help make the transition into adulthood: a journey to the Mountains in order to receive guidance from a realm which penetrates to the heart of the Tao. This ceremony helped clarify a youth's life purpose and bring The Wanderer home to rest in the Mountains.

The tendency in our culture to prolong adolescence far into adulthood is often because The Wanderer has never been properly understood. Fire, burning without a home, continually casts a spell of enchantment on the external world and leads one on an endless search for meaning and peace of mind. The next valley, the next town, the next state are all more alluring than one's own home. In order to bring Fire down from the Mountains, we must be willing to sacrifice something of our own pettiness and need for entertainment. We must be willing to quest with strength and purpose for the deeper meaning of life. If this inner Fire is ignited by our own willingness to ask for a greater vision, then The Wanderer can return home and rest.

This is the hexagram of the adolescent. There is a time for wandering and learning from the multitude of reflections in the universe, and there is a time for the Promethean task of bringing Fire down from the Mountains. All too often people choose to wander rather than suffer the difficulty of really forging a true purpose in their lives.

In search of a true home, we wander…

186

Wandering cannot last forever.
There is a time of coming home,
a time of return
and connection with the core of life.
A Gentle Wind takes us ever inwards…

57

The Gentle (Wind, Wood)

Wind moves unseen in the Heavens
and yet it carries the Waters of
the world.
Constant in its effect,
penetrating in its application,
the Wind embraces
all the Earth
and yet is gentle enough
to be a newborn's breath.
Gently contacting the facets
of our lives
we penetrate to the essence of
the Tao.

Entering
Continuous
Gentle

The Gentle (Wind, Wood)

Wind above: Penetration, Gentleness   **Wind below: Penetration, Gentleness**

Wind, blowing across the Heavens, soon clears the sky of clouds. The gentle but continual action of the Wind penetrates in all directions and blankets the Earth. The breath of life sustains every being individually and yet is universal in its effect.

Wood penetrates the Earth to draw forth moisture and nutrients in order to form a tree. Going deeply into matter waters the roots of our being. This drawing up of the primal forces of the Earth and giving them expression is the life-long task of inner development. For this action to be successful, it must be gentle. Oftentimes we wrench the substances of the Earth from the planet and build poisons rather than life. If we had but the patience to penetrate to the heart of life, then the forms we bring into being would be of service to life instead of destroying it.

The gentleness of the heart penetrates discord and conflict, and heals the wounds of our lives. This Wind of love moves, unseen, through our lives awaiting our response. In every gesture and every action, we have the possibility of giving form to our love. A flute player must provide a steady and gentle flow of breath to create music: blow too hard and the flute cannot respond, blow too little and nothing can be heard. The purest notes arrive on the most even of breaths.

Resistance is the consequence of force. Gently touching the boundaries of our souls, we can share a single breath. Struggling to make contact or pull forth nourishment, we alienate and violate the sanctity of the heart. The gentle rhythm of the breath is a resting place of tranquility. Returning to our breath, we can still the most turbulent of thoughts and penetrate to the heart of any issue. This equanimity is not static; it moves freely like the Winds, and touches many lives and many situations.

The flow of life into all forms is the essence of the Gentle Wind. Warmth and nourishment circulate on the wings of gentleness. This tender bringing forth of life awakens the heart and heals countless wounds of our past. Cultivating gentleness in our daily habits is a powerful remedy for the anger and aggression of old hurts. The Winds of change are always blowing through our lives, so why resist their contact? It may be that the next breath is the breath of a new way of being. The gentle guidance of our breath is an ever-present reminder of the penetration of the universal into the particular. The air we breathe has been shared by all of mankind for all of history. What greater symbol of the common bonds of our hearts?

The breath of our common experience is the Wind of gentleness…

189

Penetrating to the essence,
we find joy.
Finding joy, we give expression
to the Heavens
like a Lake reflecting the sky:
The Joyous Lake...

58

The Joyous (Lake)

Held in the arms of the Earth,
a Lake rejoices
moving with depth and fullness,
reflecting the Heavens
and celebrating
the dance of Wind
upon its Waters.
The ripple of life across
our hearts is the
song of the creation
being sung.

Reflection
Expression
Celebration

The Joyous (Lake)

Lake above: Joy   **Lake below: Joy**

Held by the Earth, a Lake is free to express its joy. Resting securely in the boundaries of the Earth, a Lake reflects the Heavens. Joy arises when fears have diminished. Trusting our boundaries, we do not have to hold ourselves in fear, and we can release our innate joy.

The Lake above nourishes the Lake below: an intermingling of Waters. Wisdom flows freely among friends and its sharing is an occasion for joy. This is symbolic of the joy which our friendships bring. Friends resting in each other, mutually supportive and yet able to maintain clearly their own form, provide the basis of families, societies, and cultures. When our boundaries are formed by devotion and receptivity, the joy of sharing is as natural as the flow of Water itself.

A Lake's expression is supported by the Earth and given shape by the depth of The Receptive. Clouds, Mountains and the Heavens reflect in the Lake in a scintillating, ever-changing display of light and Water. The reflections of joy enhance the contact of Heaven and Earth, and give variety and inspiration to our lives.

The Joyous Lake is symbolic of creative expression. The rendering of the world in a Lake's surface is equivalent to an artist's canvas, a musician's tapestry of music, or a dancer's definition of space. Art which has joy as its foundation is a celebration of life. The sacred can be reflected in the Waters of life and can become visible in our daily routines. The ways of the Heavens are often too subtle to be seen directly, and need to be reflected in our creative expression to become evident.

It is important to support our joy with strength. Joy without this foundation can degenerate into an escape from life instead of an expression of life. Humor which wounds instead of heals is a revelation of pain which violates the heart. Ridicule, sarcasm, and intimidation are the poison of humor which attempts to hide wounds instead of bringing relief. Humor which is gentle in movement and true in its reflection leads us to a joy which awakens the heart.

Our heart's song is joy…

Joyful expression releases constraint
and removes inhibition.
This movement of life
is the secret to Dissolution…

192

59

Dissolution

The penetrating power of truth dissolves our limitations
and releases our spirit.
A rigid heart judges and does not yield,
a gentle heart penetrates and unites,
dissolving differences.
Wind can stir the Waters
and purify our intention.
This Wind is the warmth of our hearts
penetrating the darkness
of our Waters and dissolving hidden fears.

Purification
Surrender
Egolessness

Dissolution

Wind above: Penetration, Gentleness   **Water below: The Abyss, Danger**

Wind over the Waters: a gentle heart dissolving the fear and danger of unconscious forces. The boundaries of our lives are often the areas of our greatest fears. Our sense of identity, long struggled for and gained from years of life-experience, is a boundary we do not easily release. And yet this very boundary is often what keeps us caught in destructive patterns and compulsive behaviors. In order to surrender to a change, our hardness of attitude must be dissolved. The Gentle Wind is symbolic of the heart of compassion which quietly reforms our boundaries and creates waves of the Tao in the Waters of our emotions.

Often this process of Dissolution is frightening, and it can feel as though one's whole world is falling apart. In order to ease this fear, it is important to look to the rituals in our lives which help reconnect us with a sacred order. The world of the traditional Native American is circumscribed by a continual series of dances, prayers and ceremonies. Within this sacred seasonal year, the individual person is able to live at peace with his or her own dissolving: a constant prayer to the Great Spirit through pottery, planting, jewelry, and the daily tasks of life. When faced with inner Dissolution, when the Spirit within can no longer be covered over by our daily concerns, then we need to gather together and reawaken the sacred through meaningful ceremony.

Water perfectly mirrors the moods of the Winds, and yet, within its depths, remains true to its own movement and flow. This is so, precisely because of its fluidity and ability to change. We are asked to cultivate this fluid motion in our own lives, and gather the strength to let the Winds of the Heavens reform our surfaces.

The Wind moving across Water cannot be turned back. We must surrender to the heart's movement, and trust that we will be carried to a more perfect expression of love. So much contention between couples is based on the hardening of boundaries that are the result of fearful contractions. Love is sometimes a torrent, but one which will ultimately stir our depths and inform us of the Tao.

Dissolving into the movement of truth, we are liberated...

When boundaries dissolve
and all forms become fluid
and ill-defined,
there arises the need
for Limitation...

60

Limitation

The Limitations of our lives
form the boundaries
of our souls.
Having boundaries,
we are able to undertake
the life-long task
of evolving
a complete hoop
of expression.
Accepting our obligations
transforms resistance
into strength and allows
us to fulfill our life's work.

Boundaries
Acceptance
Dharma

Limitation

Water above: The Abyss, Danger   Lake below: Joy

A Lake limits the amount of Water it can contain, and thereby gives form to the flowing Water which fills its heart. Limits are essential if we are to create structure in our lives. Water flows endlessly from the sea to the sky to the Earth and back to the sea. In this continual cycle of change, it is the limits that the Earth imposes which give character to the Water and help determine its function.

As we touch the Waters of life, we need appropriate limits in order to have the strength necessary for our journey. Water eventually washes away most boundaries; so the limits we set must be in accordance with our destiny or else they will give way during times of flood. Limits which reflect our duty in life are continually renewed by our ongoing manifestation. Limits which are too severe cripple and ultimately lead to a collapse. Limits which are too loose cannot contain the flow and are just as dangerous.

The Chinese word for "limitations" is associated with the joints that divide a bamboo stalk. Walking in a bamboo forest, the sky is lost in the dense growth of tall, firm stalks. The strength of bamboo is such that a single stalk can reach the Heavens and yet is supple enough to ripple with the passing Winds. Strengthened by our Limitations, we can remain fluid and supple. It is only when we resist essential limits that we become brittle and hardened.

When confronted with a situation which feels severely limiting, it is important to do the necessary internal work. If we push against authority and structure with willfulness and egotism, then we become weak and enslave ourselves to the very force we resist. Internalizing our Limitations, we can continually strengthen until the outer situation no longer affects us. Traditionally, monasteries and jails have always had similar schedules; one leads towards enlightenment while the other imprisons. The difference is in the inner work accomplished.

The Lake is able to reflect much greater vistas because of its limits. Streams and rivers do not have the same purity of reflection because they are in constant motion. The stillness we cultivate through discipline allows truth to become apparent.

We are liberated by our constraints…

196

Following the path of constraint
we discipline ourselves
and are made ready
to become vessels of Inner Truth...

61

Inner Truth

A Wind stirs the Lake
and makes visible the hidden
movement of the spirit.
Inner Truth brings forth change
by the purity of its own action
and its effects are often
transforming.
The constancy of a pure heart
reveals a mind free
from prejudice.
Mastering Inner Truth
we are receptive
to direct guidance
from the Tao.

Purity
Inspiration
Dependability

Inner Truth

Wind above: Penetration, Gentleness   Lake below: Joy

At the center is the unknown. Symmetry and balance surround the opening. Only with such balance can we open the floodgates to truth, for truth is often greater than our own understanding. When we touch the truth we must approach with gentleness and joy. If we approach with arrogance and pride, then we run the risk of collapse, for truth must be steadied by purity and strength if we are to make essential contact.

The Wind which blows across the Lake can play at will, for the Lake is rooted in the Earth and will not be stirred beyond its limits. The boundaries of the Earth form the crucible which allows the most subtle of truths to register. The Gentle Wind touching the Joyous Lake: this is the dance of Truth.

For the unseen to become manifest, the center must be still. Cultivating the depth of the feminine within, we strengthen the masculine without. Yielding in our hearts to the gentle Winds of guidance, we dance with joy. Profound truth incubates within and gradually reforms the body of its expression. By daily contemplation of the truth, we are asking to be remade. With gentleness and joy we undertake the great work.

Balanced within and without, we can turn towards others and recognize their truths as well. Such symmetry renders the world into a perfect hall of mirrors; everywhere we go we see the truth within as the truth without. Dancing with one another, we find the center between us is the same as the center within our own hearts. Balance in relationship steadies the ego and unlocks the mysteries which eternally call to be understood.

Contemplate the unknown, consider the space which rests between the breaths, and awaken the current of joy and gentleness which is the heart's birthright. The effect of truth is pervasive, wafting on the Winds to touch receptive hearts everywhere. The effect is powerful, yet often barely visible, and reminds us of the mystery which awaits within.

From within the center of our lives, Truth is constantly available…

In giving expression to our
Inner Truth
it is important to do so slowly
so as not to fly too high.
And so, we have Preponderance of the Small…

62

Preponderance of the Small

The nest is home to the far-flying bird
and is woven by the details
of the small things in nature.
The commonplace is the
cauldron of miracles
and it is only when we
can relax in our daily routines
that we are able to
ascend into the subtle reams
of the spirit.
Gathering strength through
our routines we
are able to
touch the Heavens.

Routine
Commonplace
Discipline

Preponderance of the Small

Thunder above: Movement, The Arousing   Mountain below: Keeping Still

Thunder in the Mountains is so immediate that it arrests our movement and demands our attention. The electrical charge prior to a lightening storm is ominous and all-pervasive. We must be aware of our surroundings; we must pay attention to our terrain if lightening is about to strike. This attention to our environment is necessary at such times. It is not a time to undertake great tasks, nor make great changes. The small and simple things of life should be our guides. "Chopping Wood and carrying Water" are the emblems of simple nourishment: they are regular disciplines that ground and stabilize our actions.

A bird which flies too high can tire, and may not have the strength to continue the journey. This is a time to come back to the nest, a time to return to the simple support of the home. The daily dignity of household chores and the worker's tasks is evident in an earthy knowledge which intuitively resolves the complex dilemmas of life. Often we strain to be free of the simple tasks of life for they feel burdensome and entrapping. Yet it is these very acts which inform us of the ways of the Tao. Without them, we run the risk of flying too high and falling prey to overwhelming moods and flights of insecure fancy.

A return to the simplicity of life is essential during times of extraordinary change. In this hexagram, the two yang lines are surrounded by four yin lines. This concentration at the center of powerful yang energy denotes an impulse of The Creative taking form in our very core. During such an extraordinary time it is best to quietly perform our daily tasks and let the Thunder fulfill its destiny.

A Mountain storm can be deadly. There is an awareness of nature that mountain-born people have which cultivates a fundamental integrity in the face of this danger. They recognize truth and resist evil. The Swiss, who have not been conquered in modern times, are examples of this mountain-born stability.

Mountain homes are often the most secure. The power of nature cultivates an appreciation of the simple strength of the home. The Mountain home must withstand Thunder, avalanche, and Wind. Only by cultivating the daily strength of simple action can such a home be built. Preponderance of the Small means a welcoming of nature's power with each task we perform.

The Power of the Small is found in our nests…

Before our journey we
"chop wood and carry water"
after our journey,
the same:
After Completion…

63

After Completion

All cycles return
to their beginnings,
all beginnings have endings,
and the changes of the Tao
eternally return.
That which has gone before
is now ahead
and the shape of the future
is a whisper in the wind.

Cycle
Return
Complete

After Completion

Water above: The Abyss, Danger   Fire below: Clarity, Perception

Fire and Water have come to a place of equilibrium. This symmetry allows necessary work to be done. Fire heats Water and produces steam; this is symbolic of the transmutation of emotions into their higher octave. Steam is a highly charged form of Water that rises to the Heavens and produces clouds. This firing of our emotional process purifies our emotions and lends strength to our lives. Balanced emotions are an essential aspect of completion. We have not truly resolved an issue until we can perceive that issue free from emotional reactivity. Having separated the clarity of our perception from the danger of our emotions is a signal of completion.

Three yin lines interpenetrate three yang lines. This balance of masculine and feminine denotes an inner harmony which signals the completion of a cycle. The stages of our growth are blessed with these plateaus. They are resting points that have been well earned. Finding a balance between creating and receiving, between strength and devotion, is a difficult task; it takes both the Fires of union and the Waters of communion to properly distill the essence of this balance.

Completion of a cycle is often a dangerous time. The culmination of a sustained period of work can often be met with exhaustion. Postpartum depression is an example of this principle at work. Often, at the moment of completion, there are already the seeds of a new cycle growing. The feeling that change is endless can be difficult to face emotionally, particularly after a long and difficult period of growth. At these times, it is important to partake fully in the nourishment of the past cycle. Fire heating Water is an image of the proper cooking of food. Eating what has been prepared will strengthen us for the next round of the cycle.

In our relationships, completing means a pause in which all that has gone before becomes clear. The balance of right and wrong, of hurt and healing, of love and dislike has established itself. This symmetry releases old patterns and allows us to see one another through fresh eyes and hearts.

Balance is the sign of completion…

What is completed
begins again.
Beginning again
happens in a time of Before Completion…

64

Before Completion

Fire flows upwards,
and Water flows downwards;
this divergence
is the threshold
of a new beginning,
a new unfolding
of the eternal
spiral of changes
which is
the Tao.

Threshold
Harmonics
New Beginnings

Before Completion

Fire above: Clarity, Perception   Water below: The Abyss, Danger

Fire moves upwards and Water flows downwards: this is the condition of Before Completion. Tendencies must be resolved in the direction of their movement in order to have completion. Fire rises to become clarity and Water descends to form our depths. Each has its own sphere of influence, and yet one is not complete without the other. Clarity, without the mystery of the unknown, borders on arrogance and limited rationality. The flow of deep emotions can be dangerous without the Fire of clear perception. Before order can be restored, Fire and Water must be accorded their proper places.

A fox walking across ice is the traditional image of this hexagram. The gait of the fox must be wary, yet steady, if it is to make it across the ice unharmed. In order to embrace the world of opposites, we must walk with a similar vigilance. The material world is a frozen sea of great potential energy. The objects of the physical world are lattices of atomic events frozen into predictable shapes. Every once in a while those events break through, and we glimpse the underlying power (the power of the atomic bomb is one example). If we are not alert, we may be swept under as the ice gives way. Diligent in our gait, we can step across the crack in the world and wander deeper into the forest. This diligence is symbolic of an attention to the environment around us. As a new century beginnings, we discover that if we are oblivious to our environment, we run the danger of drowning in the pollution of an industrial society that is no longer walking softly like a fox. We must learn to walk gently once again upon the Earth.

Before Completion is a time of exploring the extremes which lie within our hearts. Tendencies which have not been understood will make completion difficult. The relentless pressure of unexamined urges will uproot even the most stable of situations. In a time of Before Completion we must walk the burning Waters of our desires and impulses. Bringing clarity to our urges, we are able to initiate a new order of creative expression with strength and purpose.

Before Completion ends the traditional order of the hexagrams in the I Ching. Sixty-four windows have opened; now, at the end of the book, we are asked to look beyond to the next cycle. We are invited to leave the books and return to the only true possible arena of completion: our own lives.

The end is always a beginning…

Guide to Using the Coin Method to Generate the Hexagrams

Three coins are thrown six times, generating a line with each throw. The Hexagram is built from the bottom to the top, so the sixth and final throw will create the top line of the Hexagram.

Two tails and a head yields a yang line: ⸻⸻

Two heads and a tail yields a yin line: ⸻ ⸻

Three heads yields a changing yang line: ⸻x⸻

Three tails yields a changing yin line: ⸻o⸻

When changing lines appear it means that two Hexagrams are being generated as an answer. The first is made up of the lines as thrown, the second is made up of the changed and unchanged lines (for example, a changing yang line becomes a yin line. If we threw all yang lines with the top line changing, our first Hexagram would be six yang lines, the second Hexagram would be made up of five yang lines, with a yin line on top).

	Ch'ien	Chên	K'an	Kên	K'un	Sun	Li	Tui
Ch'ien	1	34	5	26	11	9	14	43
Chên	25	51	3	27	24	42	21	17
K'an	6	40	29	4	7	59	64	47
Kên	33	62	39	52	15	53	56	31
K'un	12	16	8	23	2	20	35	45
Sun	44	32	48	18	46	57	50	28
Li	13	55	63	22	36	37	30	49
Tui	10	54	60	41	19	61	38	58

Lower Trigram

Chart of the Trigrams and Hexagrams

211

About the Author

The depth of David LaChapelle's vision and selfless service began in his youth, nurtured among the natural beauty of glaciers and mountains with his parents Dolores and Ed LaChapelle. Later, under the guidance of Lakota medicine man John Fire Lame Deer, he was steeped in Native American practices and began to broaden the lens of his connection to patterns of metaphysical and ceremonial realms.

Following his formative years, David journeyed to Baba Muktananda's ashram in India, beginning in-depth yogic studies he would continue throughout his life. He would also delve deeply into the wells of Western psychology, body-oriented therapies, scientific inquiry and artistic expression.

An active artist, humble musician and bard, lover of nature, and dear teacher to many, David was a tireless weaver of the seemingly separate mystical traditions and devotional cultures of the world. He offered students crisp revelation and contextual understanding for the more subtle states of consciousness, and effective, individualized practices for accessing each student's own unique connection to the Divine. David actively led groups and guided individuals into realms of spiritual insight for over thirty years.

David LaChapelle passed from his body in Durango, Colorado on July 21st of 2009 of pneumonia following several months of chemotherapy for throat cancer. His partner, fellow artist and "transition midwife" Ananda Elise Foley, maintains a website marketplace for David's creative publications: www.umya.com, as well as a blogsite celebrating his cherished life at http://celebratingdavid.blogspot.com

Other Pulications by David LaChapelle

Destiny Lines. Sounds True, 2003. ISBN-10: 1591790050; ISBN-13: 978-1591790051

Navigating the Tides of Change: Stories From Sience, the Sacred, and a Wise Planet. New Society Publishers, 2001. Gabriola Island, Canada. ISBN: 0-86571-424-X

A Voice on the Wind: A Fable About Coming of Age. Gateway Productions, 1995. Juneau, AK, USA. ISBN: 1-887217-01-0

Mountains of Light & Pathways of Love: A Fable About Love, Death and Marriage. Gateway Productions, 1993. Juneau, AK, USA. ISBN:

The Storyteller's Mirror: Ordinary People and Their Extraordinary Reflections. Wind Over Mountain Press, 1991. Juneau AK, USA.

David's website: **www.umya.com** offers a marketplace for his expression of artwork, writing, and eventually, recordings and transcripts of workshop talks.

LaVergne, TN USA
10 December 2009
166276LV00002BB